curtains
a design source book

curtains
a design source book

Caroline Clifton-Mogg

photography by
James Merrell

RYLAND
PETERS
& SMALL
LONDON NEW YORK

First published in the USA in 1997

This revised edition published in 2005

by Ryland Peters & Small, Inc.

519 Broadway

5th Floor

New York, NY 10012

www.rylandpeters.com

10 9 8 7 6 5 4 3 2 1

Library of Congress Cataloging-in-Publication Data

Clifton-Mogg, Caroline.

    Curtains / by Caroline Clifton-Mogg ; photography by
James Merrell.

        p. cm. (A design source book)

    Includes index.

    ISBN 1-84172-932-9

    1. Drapery—Handbooks, manuals, etc. I. Title. II.
Series.

NK3195.C62   1997

747' . 5–dc21   97-12775

Illustrations **Jacqueline Pestell**, **Amanda Patton**

Stylist **Melanie Molesworth**

For this edition:

Designer **Luana Gobbo**

Senior Editor **Henrietta Heald**

Picture Research **Emily Westlake**

Production **Gemma Moules**

Art Director **Gabriella Le Grazie**

Publishing Director **Alison Starling**

The first edition of this book was designed by
Ingunn Jensen and edited by Caroline Davison,
with location research by Nadine Bazar.

Printed and bound in China.

Contents

FOREWORD

After the great curtain overload of the 1980s—all those voluminous lengths of material, weighed down with swags and cascades, tassels and tiebacks—there was, not surprisingly, a backlash. A new attitude took hold in interior design. Fussy curtains were pulled down and consigned to the attic or thrift store, and windows were dressed with very simple curtains, or even no curtains at all. But that reaction against the excesses of the past is now over, and people are once again taking pleasure in choosing and using all sorts of drapery and design.

Curtains and shades are practical objects, valuable for keeping in the warmth and keeping out the light, but they are also—as they have always been—an integral element of interior decoration. Just as important as the style of furniture or the color of the walls are the curtains you choose. Their texture and design, color and pattern are part of the essentials that make a successful room. They add a necessary softness and fluidity whose absence would render the best-designed rooms hard and cold.

The first edition of *Curtains: A Design Source Book* aimed to help you find your way through the huge variety of window treatments available, suggesting the simplest and most successful ways of dressing different windows, whatever their shape or size. This new edition brings the interior design information contained in the original right up to date. It includes more than 100 new photographs, showing even more imaginative ideas and examples of how and where to use curtains and shades.

Caroline Clifton-Mogg

BELOW, RIGHT, FAR RIGHT *Heavy, carved and gilded wooden cornices often surmounted equally heavy draperies. Here, in a Victorian house in London, a double-depth cornice is used with a traditional portière. Unusually, there are two draperies rather than one: the outer drapery is caught up with an ornamental rope while the lighter inner one is held back by a bracket hidden behind the outer draperies.*

Influential Styles

Taste, as commentators know to their cost, is almost impossible to define. In any group, taste is both personal and communal, formed not only by the influences on any one individual but also by the more general influences of society. In this time of instant communication, when we have immediate access to a wealth of inspirational sources, it is becoming increasingly difficult to define our personal tastes. This is why the styles of the past, particularly of draperies that reflect the interior decoration of a period so accurately, should be regarded as a well-stocked library of decorative treasures through which we can browse in search of inspiration. Indeed, the early 20th-century decorator John Fowler, who was renowned for his imaginative window treatments, gained much inspiration from 18th-century dress, and many were the draperies and swags to which he added a braided detail from an embroidered silk vest or a ruffle from a taffeta skirt. So let us document, briefly, the threads of fashion that, throughout the ages, have influenced, and can still lead to, new drapery styles.

As with every aspect of art, some periods have been more fruitful than others. Indeed, throughout the last few hundred years there has been imagination in drapery design from which we can draw inspiration as well as pleasure. Historically speaking, however, draperies have not always been perceived as a decorative element. In fact, it was not until humans had passed the stage of merely surviving that an appreciation of the beautiful in the natural world as well as in fine and decorative arts began to develop. Early householders had more pressing concerns, chief among them being how best to keep the cold and damp at bay. Textiles in the house were hung on the walls and around the bed rather than at the window—for practical rather than decorative reasons. But a love of decoration for its own sake is innate in humankind, and gradually even the early wall and bed hangings became richly ornate.

Draperies first became prominent as an essential element in interior decoration in 16th-century Europe. Inspiration came, as always at that time, from France and Italy, and the influence of these two bastions of fashion would be felt in England and the Low Countries some time afterward.

The first draperies were single; pairs came later. The simplest consisted of strips of fabric, sometimes of basic weave and construction, somewhat like the natural curtain and drapery styles popular today. But other draperies were more flamboyant and made from velvets from Genoa or heavy brocades and silks from Venice. By the 17th century, earlier technical

problems in glazing windows had mainly been solved, and windows gradually became larger.

In England the draperies that hung at these vast windows were still rather basic, but elsewhere in Europe both window draperies and bed hangings became increasingly more elaborate. For example, the French designer Daniel Marot published ideas for extravagantly decorated beds which included huge drapes and swags, plumes and tassels, in an excess of richness. To a certain extent, the ideas of Marot and his contemporaries still influence decorative designs for headboards and canopies today, albeit in a simpler and, usually, more graceful form.

Beginning in 1700, a multiplicity of drapery styles began to appear, including the festoon curtain, which was the forerunner of our modern balloon or Austrian shade. When designed correctly and made in the right weight of material, these shades are a striking solution for a tall window.

As with every other aspect of interior decoration and the decorative arts, the 18th century is, for many, the period when drapery design reached a standard that was never to be bettered. Combining wit, imagination, and elegance, the draperies were relatively simple, straight, and made from beautiful materials. They hung from cornices and valances whose ornamentation added to the whole effect and are still a yardstick by which to measure contemporary designs. Indeed, many of the styles and ideas proposed by architects and upholsterers of the time continue to influence modern draperies.

During the latter half of the 18th century and the early 19th century, the neoclassical style became extremely popular. It remains so today in various forms. The first excavations of the lava-covered cities of Pompeii and Herculaneum in Italy also took place at this time. The paintings and mosaics on the walls and floors of the ancient houses in the ruins sparked off a long-lasting enthusiasm for classical architecture and decoration in Europe and America. From this period came drapery poles adorned with finials in the form of spears, laurel wreaths, and other militaristic or classical motifs which are popular today.

The influence of the 18th-century Scottish designer Robert Adam, who was inspired by classical designs and motifs, remains great. He treated the draperies and surrounding archi-trave, or window molding, particularly for the tall windows popular at the time, in a rela-tively simple way with restrained swags and cascades or folded draw shades, which often fell from carved and gilded cornice boards made of wood or plaster. All these ideas can be used in narrow-windowed rooms today.

By the end of the 18th century, French-influenced draw curtains with a draped valance had also become popular. They had a flowing line in which the material draped and billowed, offering opportunities for invention and inspiration. These draperies were made from lighter fabrics such as silks and cottons, taffetas and satins. No longer were draperies simply a means of controlling light: the dress curtain had arrived. Hung beneath valances in different designs, these draw draperies flowed from beneath a richly carved cornice board.

By the early 19th century the neoclassical look was refined again. It became heavier,

even ponderous, losing much of the lightness of touch that had been associated with Robert Adam. Great emphasis was placed on the decorative elements of design, in particular on the style of the valances, and swags and cascades. In fact, *passementerie*—all those lovely handmade fringes, tassels, braids, and rosettes—was as popular then as it is today.

LEFT, ABOVE, RIGHT *Nearly all styles of curtain are influenced by what has gone before. In this bedroom in France, the classically inspired painted wooden bed is curtained in 18th-century style, two curtains falling from a central canopy. A charming, restrained balloon shade has been made from the same material, and in the dressing room, a sheer muslin has been loosely draped to follow the lines of both bed and window.*

curtain or drapery at the window or several different sheers draped over a rod has a new relevance and can create very informal effects at windows.

However, by the 19th century the well-mannered simplicity of the past had gone. In both Europe and America the past was mined for inspiration, and earlier styles were revived with abandon—from the medieval to the Elizabethan, from Scottish Baronial to Louis X1V and Louis XV—and often used together. With this approach to style came a belief that a little more of everything was desirable. Drapery styles became rich in the extreme: so grand, so excessive, so much. New chemical dyes led to stronger, even harsher, colors, while window treatments consisting of heavy swags and cascades, outer draperies, inner draperies, sheer curtains, and often shades made from Holland linen were not unusual. No part of a room's architecture, including doorways, mantelpieces, and alcoves, remained free from drapery. If you wish to dress a window extravagantly, make sure that the finished design conveys a sense of vibrancy rather than of unbridled excess.

Toward the end of the 19th century, an inevitable reaction to the frills and fuss of High Victoriana took place, a development embodied by the Arts and Crafts movement. Designers and architects such as William

ABOVE, RIGHT In this modestly decorated room, the windows exhibit a simplified version of an often elaborate style. Plain fabric is draped in an informal swag over a small window. Another piece of fabric is arranged in a swag attached to the ceiling beams. Beneath this, a floor-length drapery is held back at sill height with a bracket.

FAR RIGHT The end of the 18th century saw a certain severity enter the decorative vocabulary. Frills and excessive ornament were eschewed in favour of purity of line. Here, against a commanding pair of windows, a sheer fabric is hung in restrained fashion, caught and gathered in a loose billow.

Drapery poles and finials often took center stage, seemingly artlessly draped with fabric in a number of imaginative ways. Two or more materials were often used at one window, combining not only different patterns but also varying textures and weights. Undercurtains of gauze or silk were also used; these either fell straight to the ground or were caught back, often in asymmetrical opposition to the accompanying draperies. Today, particularly with the wide selection of sheer fabrics now available, ranging from silk to synthetics, the idea of using more than one lightweight

Morris and Philip Webb advocated natural simplicity, whereby ornament became secondary to the object, not its *raison d'être*. They mocked the excesses of contemporary interior-decoration, and over the next few decades their ideas took hold, and rich, heavy furnishings became less common. Events far removed from design and decoration also influenced stylistic developments. During World War I, ornate draperies were regarded as impractical, and simpler designs, which were easier to keep clean and fresh, started to replace them. Following the war, such decorators as Nancy Lancaster, Sibyl Colefax, and John Fowler made a virtue of simplicity and began to decorate in what is now recognized as the style of the "English country house": comfortable, informal, and with relatively simpler, freer draperies.

Today, technical advances in fiber production and in printing have made the options almost infinite. So, whether you prefer restrained 18th-century-inspired narrow draperies, full-blown draperies and swags, unlined muslin and silk suspended from a wooden pole, or even electronically controlled Venetian blinds, all is possible, all is attainable.

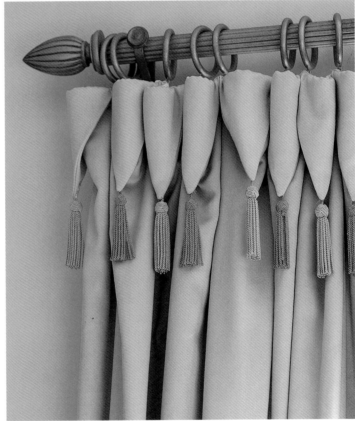

LEFT, ABOVE *These relatively simple draperies are a contemporary version of a popular Regency design. The ornamental reeded brass pole is typical of many early 19th-century designs, while the shape of the finials can be seen in many neoclassic illustrations. A drapery heading of elongated handkerchief points, edged with tassels in two colors, emphasizes the curves of the finials.*

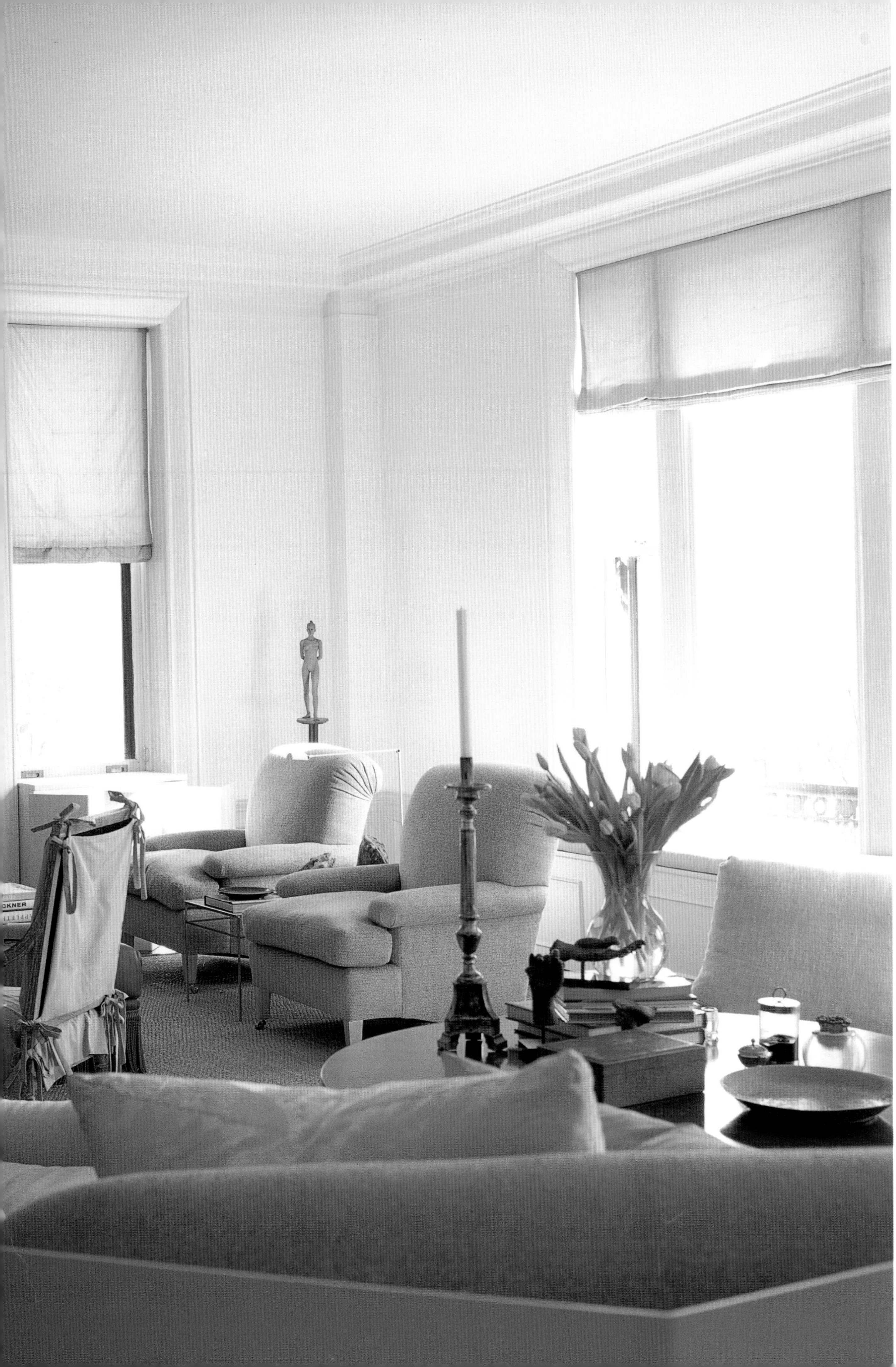

Window Style

WINDOW STYLE

Whether conventionally beautiful or simply practical, every window has a unique character that is integral to the architectural style and interior design of the house. People need light and air, and when they enter a room for the first time, their eyes are usually drawn to the window, whether it is dressed with traditional draperies; shades made from fabric, wood, metal, plastic, or paper; fretwork, paper, or trellis screens; painted stencils; or even climbing plants. But it is only by standing back and looking at your uncovered windows that you will be able to study their shape and assess their individual merits and needs. Whatever the size of the window, it should be dressed to look as appealing as possible and never hidden beneath a torrent of fabric. Instead, the window should remind you of a beautiful woman at a party whose understated gown ensures everyone finds her as enchanting as her dress.

ABOVE *These windows are dressed as one, in such a way that they dominate the room. The sheer draperies are caught back in a deep loop at the same point as the heavier outer draperies. The effect would not be so successful were it not for the obelisk which draws the windows together.*

RIGHT *As this drapery, which is mainly plain except for the plaid heading, shows, a drapery can also be used to good effect on a wall.*

RIGHT *An awkwardly placed window such as this, which reaches into the corner of the room, leaves little space for draperies on either side or even above. However, the draperies, which are slotted over a shiny metal pole through oversized metal eyelets, are particularly arresting. The area is made more interesting by the mirrored wall, which emphasizes the window treatment by doubling its size. The elegant chair in front of the window blends in color with the draperies.*

Tall Windows

A tall window, especially one of fine proportions, is an object of style. Particularly associated with the Georgian architecture and style of the 18th century—a period commonly acknowledged to have epitomized all that is elegant in decoration—such windows are a perfection of design. If any of your rooms has classic proportions and is blessed with tall windows, you are lucky indeed, and a variety of styles can be yours.

In British Georgian houses the tallest windows are usually found on the second floor. Traditionally known as the *piano nobile*, this is

where the formal reception rooms were situated. Today, such rooms and windows offer bounteous opportunities for both traditional, formal treatments and simpler designs. Treatments for tall windows should concentrate on maximizing the available light. This is perhaps obvious, but in an enthusiasm for complicated designs it is sometimes ignored. So, even if yours is a very tall window in a classically proportioned room, show some restraint in your choice of drapery style, and avoid draperies, valances, swags and cascades, or cornice boards that are too heavy or ornate.

Although a tight, restrained look is chic, narrow draperies must be made with enough

ABOVE, ABOVE LEFT *The whole of this tall, narrow window is dressed with a single drapery panel, caught back with a rope that is attached to the window frame. The shape of this window offers an ideal opportunity to use a piece of old textile, in this case an antique paisley shawl, and provides a perfect frame for the deep border and traditional motifs.*

FAR LEFT, TOP CENTER *This tall window butts up to a wood-clad ceiling, and so the drapery heading is necessarily a simple one. A wrought-iron pole is fixed directly to the bare wood, and the draperies are hung from rings that are attached to the deceptively simple fold-over heading. The blue ribbons, which pick out the color of the draperies, are tied into bows in front of each ring.*

fabric to make their fullness look intentionally restricted rather than the result of parsimony. If you have a period house, consider when it was built and how the original owners would have treated the windows. What could be more appropriate than a pair of classic draperies headed with a simple swag and cascades or a single panel draped diagonally across the window frame and caught high up with a tieback or a metal bracket? This last treatment is also a smart way to dress a window with interior shutters.

If you would prefer not to have a valance or swags and cascades at a tall window, then the type and depth of the drapery heading you choose is of the utmost importance. You can opt for basic pinch pleats, formed with special pleat tape and hooks, or drawstrings, or you can indulge your taste for elegance with a hand-sewn heading in one of a variety of styles, from the simple to the elaborate. Unless you are confident of your measuring and sewing skills, however, a complex design should be entrusted to a professional. Fortunately, many of the most fashionable headings are simple, with the fabric softly pleated or even left flat, and well within the capabilities of an amateur.

BELOW LEFT *Here, where there is no wall space between the windows and the ceiling molding and where the windows also extend to the very corners of the room, only the simplest treatment is possible, with the draperies suspended by rings from an unadorned iron pole.*

BOTTOM LEFT *This room has a "dead" space above the window, although the draperies hanging below the pole give an illusion of space.*

BELOW *Here, there is little space between the fairly thick architrave and ceiling. To minimize bulk, the draperies are flat panels, hung by brass grommets from a specially designed, gently undulating pole. The effect is soft yet striking.*

The section of the window from which you hang draperies or curtains always requires some thought, particularly with a tall window, because a rod hung in the wrong position can alter its proportions, sometimes for the worse. The usual choice is on the architrave or just above, but if the rod is hung above the window, you should make sure that no molding or cornice is obscured. Ideally, as in most old houses, there is often a section of wall between the top of the window frame and the cornice, known in Britain as the deadlight. However, in badly converted or modern

ABOVE *This badly proportioned window with no space above it has been salvaged by hanging the draperies from a metal pole and attaching a wide swath of fabric which is deliberately allowed to sag in the center. This creates an attractive, draped effect that draws the eye away from the area above the window.*

FAR RIGHT *A tall, narrow window in a paneled room is hung with a single, striped drapery from a classical pole. The unususal textile with a thick black border, which flows over much of the drapery, not only breaks up its height but is also an original decorative device.*

versions of classic rooms, there is often no such space. In this case, the proportions of both window and drapery should be righted optically if not physically after the rod has been attached. This can sometimes be done with a valance or cornice that, rather than cutting horizontally across the window, follows the window down on either side, thus bringing the eye downward too. A plain, full-height, translucent shade that hangs from beneath the draperies will also anchor the window and prevent it appearing to float in the wall space.

One way to allow as much light as possible through a tall window, while still showing off its fine lines, is to use a draw-up blind. These were originally popular in the 17th and 18th centuries, when windows began to sport festoon curtains, made in translucent materials such as muslin or silk or in damask or figured silk. Such shades were hung either beneath formal stationary panels or from a cornice board made from carved and gilded wood or plaster. These elegant panels were also eminently practical because they could be drawn up underneath the cornice in order to allow in the maximum amount of light.

The modern balloon shades are far less dignified, however. In Britain they are often referred to derogatorily as "knicker [panty] blinds," because of the preponderance of overly large frills. Balloon shades today are all too often seen hanging against unsuitably shaped windows, which are either too wide, too small, or too tall, and are often made from inappropriate fabrics and in unsuitable designs. It is a shame that this style is so badly handled when it still has a perfectly useful role to play under the right circumstances, namely at a tall window where space is limited. In short, if you employ a treatment that is in itself elaborate, no embellishment to the basic shape is really necessary. The basic shape of the shade itself should be simple, with the trimmings kept to a minimum. When you pull

ABOVE *The proportions of a window that is not full height can be improved by designing a special window treatment. Here, narrow draperies are tied back at sill height, which carries the eye downward, as does the gently curved valance. This gives the draperies more impact than the window.*

BELOW *A badly proportioned window is corrected with a witty treatment in which the draperies fold over a loose rope secured by brackets. This draws the attention away from the window, while the way in which the draperies flow over the floor balances the weight at ceiling level.*

All this advice holds true for perfectly proportioned windows, but sadly, in an often less than ideal decorative world, even such seemingly simple features as a window of perfect proportions are hard to find. Windows are often too narrow, too wide, or simply too tall for the height of the room. In such cases, care must be taken to balance any proportional problems in order to achieve the best effects. If the window is too narrow, the simplest solution is to extend the rod beyond the window frame so that the draperies hang against the wall rather than the architrave. Tall, narrow windows can be made to look wider with the addition of louvered or paneled shutters which, when not in use, hinge backward so that they rest flat against the walls on each side of the window rather than folding back into the recess.

A tall, narrow window does not, of course, always extend to floor level. If this is your situation make sure that you use the draperies to correct this by taking the draperies to floor level and maybe using a contrasting band of fabric at the bottom of each panel. You could also paint a panel on the dead area of wall above the floor. Both these treatments have the effect of anchoring and extending the window.

Narrow windows on the same wall can be dressed to look wider, while still admitting the maximum amount of light, by adding a false valance. This is achieved by attaching a valance or an arrangement of swags to the draperies themselves rather than to the window frame. When the draperies are opened, the valances draw back with them; when closed, they look like richly dressed hangings.

However, not every pair of draperies at a tall window needs to open. Indeed, if you have a tall window on a landing or at a turn in the stairs, carefully draped stationary panels left permanently in their show position will look much better than draperies that are constantly being adjusted.

ABOVE *A pair of narrow windows, one of which runs almost up to the corner of the room, are dressed in a way that corrects any imperfection in their proportions while being compatible with the elegant and restrained style of the rest of the room. False valances have been used to good effect; when closed, the deep valance gives the window area elegance and style, but when the curtains are drawn back, maximum daylight is obtained.*

down the shade on a tall window, make sure that the area on display is in proportion to that of the window below. Another option for such a well-proportioned window is a flat-pleated Roman shade which is usually hung within the window frame, its horizontal fold lines displaying the architecture of the window.

BELOW, RIGHT, FAR RIGHT *A simple, intrinsically uninteresting window is made to look both wider and more important by a dramatic window treatment which also allows maximum light to enter the room. Behind the pole, a curtain made from a sheer yellow fabric is slipped over a curtain rod and then caught back by a hidden tieback. The heavier drapery, which is suspended from the pole, is arranged to produce a narrow, more formal drape.*

FAR LEFT, LEFT, ABOVE *This is a contemporary version of a classic window treatment in which a modern fabric design with wide, strongly colored stripes hangs from beneath an ornate, gilded cornice. This gives the drapery as much weight as the cornice. These are particularly well-chosen draperies for landings because they add much to the lines of the staircase as well as promote a feeling of security and comfort.*

Wide Windows

Improvements in glass-making technology over the past few centuries have made possible a huge variety of window styles. In the 17th and 18th centuries, windows were composed of many small panes, and it was not until the introduction of plate glass in the 19th century that window sashes made of a single large pane could be manufactured. As glazing costs fell, windows grew wider as well as taller.

Wide or large windows made from several panes of glass can be treated in a different manner from those used for single-paned windows. For example, multipaned windows can be effectively dressed with blinds or shades or hung with floor-length draperies. You can also introduce some contrast within the glazing by using opaque glass for some of the panes in order to produce an abstract design.

The treatment of large picture windows can be problematic. If the house is secluded, it may be possible to leave such a window uncovered, so as to bring the view into the room. But if your neighbors have a view of you, some form of curtaining is vital. This also helps to conserve heat and reduce fading of carpets and furniture. The trick is to achieve this without suggesting that the "big show" is about to begin.

One of the first considerations is whether you want the draperies to be full length or sill length. Once again, it is a question of proportion: width must always be balanced by height, and if the window is wider than it is high, the width should be balanced with sufficient fabric length below the window—or even with fabric extended above the window. If you need to break up the glazed area visually, two or three flat, pleated Roman shades or an equal number of roller shades that are set at different heights along the window should have the desired effect.

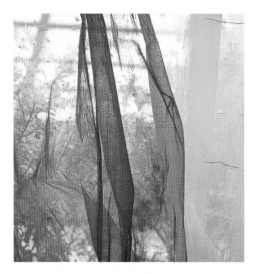

OPPOSITE (left, below right) *Wide windows often present problems of proportion, especially if they do not extend from the ceiling to the floor. Here, a shallow wide window is dressed with two Roman shades. These are set at different heights for variety and interest. Made of sheer fabric, the Roman shades can be kept partially raised at any level across the width of the window. This treatment is successful because it breaks up what would otherwise be a rather unattractive expanse of glass. The border stitched down the sides and along the bottom of each shade is almost the same width as the dark window frames. This creates a highly harmonious effect.*

BELOW, LEFT, OPPOSITE (above right) *Typical picture windows can be overwhelming by virtue of their sheer size, particularly when they occupy two walls. The clever solution devised here turns a series of windows into an ethereal fantasy with sheer gauzelike draperies in wide rainbow-colored stripes. These draperies fall in a relaxed, unstructured fashion, and billow in the breeze. The informality of the treatment is emphasized further by the almost casual heading style of the curtains. This consists of pieces of string tied into loose decorative bows. The effect is one of impermanence that suits the relaxed atmosphere of the room.*

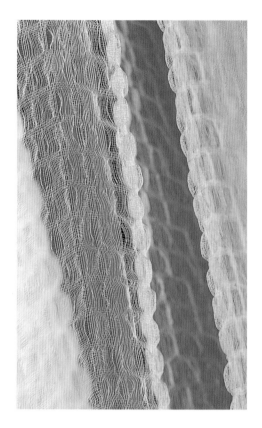

Similarly, if you would like to diminish the area of a window, you could use a lambrequin, which, somewhat like an extended valance, runs down either side of the window as well as across the top. By positioning the lambrequin over a section of the window, you can lessen the area of glass visible from inside the room.

If you have a wide window, it is tempting to hang an elaborate confection of swags and cascades across the top. Try not to succumb to this temptation. First, it is difficult to successfully design an arrangement of swags across such a wide area, and second, you should really try to focus attention on the view offered by such an expanse of glass rather than on the draperies around the view. Simplicity in this case is definitely the best approach. If the view is beautiful, consider having the curtains blend with the color of the walls, so that the landscape, not the interior decoration, becomes predominant.

Whatever your view, however, the design of fabric for any large expanse of glass, whether it is composed of a single window or the entire width so that a diffusion of, or even a mere suggestion of, the world outside is all that permeates. For example, muslin or a fine voile looks good, particularly if it has a woven rather than printed design. Decorative lace, with its delicacy and intricate detail, would be less successful over a large window area—a little of such a fabric goes a long way. A more flexible alternative would be to fix a sequence of paper screens across the window. These would not only diffuse the light but also break up the space occupied by the glass.

OPPOSITE (bottom, top left, top center) *The drapery fabric at these wide windows has a strong surface interest. The heavy, rippled fabric is used in profusion to create sculptural folds. The severity of the treatment is softened by the gentle puddling of the draperies on the floor.*

BELOW, LEFT, OPPOSITE (top right) *These wide windows are hung with draperies made from a dimpled, plastic fabric. The draperies are headed with pleats that are seemingly held together with ties and run on a barely visible rod.*

a group of windows, should be chosen with care. It should be neither too subdued nor too elaborate, because a design that is charming over an average-sized space can be a disaster when repeated ad infinitum. Small, indeterminate prints, stripes, or plaids simply will not work. Large windows call for equally large and flamboyant designs, whether they be naturalistic, abstract, geometric, or striped.

Solid-colored fabrics work well, but if the expanse to be covered is exceptionally large, a drapery would probably look better if it is defined by wide, contrasting borders that run down the edges or across the lower edge. A valance or cornice will also add definition to draperies made from solid-colored fabric. Of course, if the view from your window is not appealing, you can use a sheer material across

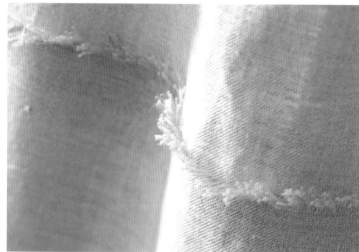

LEFT, ABOVE, RIGHT *Tall, wide windows often need an optical illusion to bring them into scale. Here, the inner draperies start some way down from the top of the window, suspended by strings fixed above the window. Righting the balance, but extending the illusion, another drapery is hung from the ceiling and reaches farther into the room. The draperies are made from wide bands of coarse material sewn together in an informal way.*

BELOW *A traditional treatment for a picture window that does not cover the length of the room is simply to extend the draperies beyond the window onto the wall itself. This simple procedure cohesively unites wall, window, and room.*

When choosing a fabric for wide windows, you should also consider how the amount of light that filters through the material will influence the whole effect. For example, a thick lining material, which admits very little light, would draw attention to the design of a drapery fabric. By contrast, unlined draperies have a slightly translucent look which can be particularly pretty when the draperies are made of such material as silk or light cotton.

Some picture windows, especially those that are situated at first floor level, are part fixed glass and part sliding door. When deciding on the type of curtains or draperies for this arrangement, you should make sure that they can be pulled back beyond the sliding mechanism of the door so that the folds of material do not get caught when you open or shut the door.

Many of the suggestions made so far apply to windows that are reasonably well proportioned. Unfortunately, there are many wide windows that have been less skillfully designed. Indeed, they seem to lack any sense of composition or proportion, simply resembling faceless expanses of glass. In addition, ill-designed wide windows are often not helped by ugly frames, usually made from metal, which are meagerly proportioned. However, badly proportioned wide windows can be corrected to some extent by the judicious use of window treatments.

FAR LEFT, LEFT, BELOW *In a bedroom, care must be taken not to overwhelm the room with the window treatment. Here, a window is visually enlarged by extending the pole and draperies beyond the sides of the window. The finished effect is not heavy, however, due to the simple design of the material and the traditional, almost anonymous, style of the drapery pole.*

OPPOSITE *Wide, shallow windows can be effectively treated with shades, particularly if they look unusual. Here, a single piece of cocoa-colored fabric, which is less formal than a traditional Roman shade, is supported by strips of ribbon tied into bows along the bottom. Decorative metal hooks provide an unusual finishing touch.*

For example, the apparent size of the window can, if necessary, be extended with headings or poles that run beyond the windows themselves so that the draperies hang down the wall on either side of the window rather than cutting into the window.

If the window is disproportionately tall, a fixed cornice board of a suitable depth would correct the height. More than two curtains could be hung from behind the board at various points to give the impression, when opened, of separate windows.

As is the case for wide windows that have perfect proportions, three or four flat, pleated shades can be used successfully to break up the area of glass, reduce the levels of light, and provide an element of privacy. Indeed, the many shade systems now available are the ideal solution for wide windows. Shades have the added advantage of being highly flexible treatments. They also vary considerably in style and price, from the relatively cheap to the extremely expensive. A low-looped, sheer Austrian shade, for example, could be pulled down permanently over part of the window, perhaps beneath a pair of draperies. This would diffuse the light and also alter the proportions of the window.

Small Windows

Many houses and apartments have small windows and, as with other windows with a distinctive shape, the first question to be asked is whether they should be covered at all. This is probably not advisable if the window is set high in the wall. Indeed, a small, uncovered window can be a decorative feature in itself, especially if the wooden frame is painted in an eyecatching, and perhaps contrasting, color. If there is a deep sill, this could also be painted to emphasize the shape of the window further.

A sense of scale is very important when dealing with small windows, and decorative ideas must be in proportion to the size of the window. You should avoid, for example, such embellishments as drooping swags and cascades or any of the other more exaggerated headings that work so well on larger windows. Headings should not be too deep, and if you are using a decorative rod, make sure that it is thin enough to match the weight and depth of the curtain or drapery. Small windows do not even need two panels. A single panel caught back to form a loop on one side of the

ABOVE *A tiny window is given a new importance with a clever treatment. A piece of material is draped from an iron pole, suspended above the window, to from a heavy swag which, although imposing, allows in the maximum amount of light.*

TOP, ABOVE LEFT *Just because a window is small does not mean it has to be dull. Here, in a charming variation of an asymmetrical Georgian swag, a floor-length, white drapery is caught back beneath the sill, which has the effect of elongating the window. The drapery is crowned with a heavy, striped material which, with its rough, scalloped edge, suggests both a valance and a classic swag and cascades.*

window is a pretty and practical idea. The drapery can be released at night or kept in place, with a plain shade to keep out the light.

Often out of proportion to the wall or room, small windows require a dextrous treatment to counteract any design fault. If, for example, the window is narrow as well as short, the drapery rod should be extended so that the draperies hang on either side of the frame. However, make sure that the rod extends only a little way on each side so that there is no wall space visible between the draperies and the window frame.

Small windows are often hung with sill-length draperies or curtains because floor-length panels usually look out of proportion. But if you are trying to correct uneven proportions, the length could be extended an inch or two below the sill; alternatively, the rod might be set slightly higher, usually without losing the sense of scale. If you do want to hang floor-length draperies over a small window, perhaps to correct the proportions of

LEFT, BELOW *Unlined draperies are ideal for small windows, particularly if there are also shutters. This pretty fabric, embroidered with a trail of flowers along the top, is tied back and draped beyond the window frame in order to maximize the amount of light in the room.*

the rest of the room, you should consider positioning both the draperies and a roller shade well above the window. The roller shade can then be pulled down to cover the exposed wall and part of the window to give the appearance of a much larger window.

If the small window is set into a recess, the window could be hung with a roller shade and the wall that opens to the recess itself might be hung with a pair of floor-length draperies. These could perhaps be made in a material that complements the blind. This gives not only the window but also the whole area a new importance. Another solution, if you have a small window set into a deep recess, is to repeat the design of the window frame

around the outer edge of the window in order to create the illusion of a much larger window. You could emphasize the effect still further by painting both the frame and the outer frame in a contrasting color.

If the small window is also rather ugly—and this applies equally to unattractive large or narrow windows—then one solution is to dress them as insignificantly as possible and to harmonize the color of the curtains or draperies with the color of the walls. Try using fabric one tone paler or darker than the color of the walls to create a harmonious look without drawing too much unwanted attention to the window. It goes without saying that the window treatment in such a case should not

BELOW LEFT *Obviously, the smaller the window, the more important it is to allow in as much light as possible, and any curtain or shade should be of the utmost simplicity. Here, a pair of red-checked dishtowels have been hung from a narrow, expanding curtain-wire rod that is attached to the edge of the window frame itself, rather than to the wall.*

BELOW *This tiny, oval window is imaginatively treated with a curtain pierced with grommets hung from a narrow rod; ornamental metal hooks are set along the top of the window frame. The result is utterly charming.*

BOTTOM *Multicolored ribbons are attached to a fixed, narrow rod set against the window itself. The architrave frames the composition.*

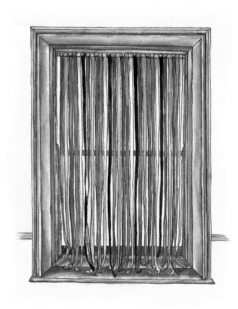

be overly elaborate. If the treatment is simple and straightforward, the curtains or draperies—and the windows themselves—will make their presence felt in only the most well-mannered of ways.

Your choice of fabric is also very important. As a rule, you should avoid heavy velvets, brocades, wools, and heavily embossed cottons. Small windows require light, airy materials which both reflect and balance their diminutive size. The same rule applies to patterned fabrics, which should be simpler in design and scale than those used at larger windows. When seen in a pattern book or in a shop, the design of a fabric, particularly if it

has a petite repeating pattern, will look much smaller than the finished curtain, drapery, or shade fitted at the window.

This is an appropriate moment to explore the advantages of using colored linings at undersized windows. Indeed, a small window curtained in fabric that has a simple, little design and a lining in one of the colors in the design, or in a soft, welcoming color such as deep pink or warm yellow, brings a feeling of comfort and coziness to the bleakest of days, seeming to change the color of the light inside the room. Such a treatment also gives the window a cheerful appearance from outside the house.

ABOVE, ABOVE LEFT *A Roman shade is one of the cleanest and neatest ways of treating a small window. Here, the shade is set within the architrave, and the edges are trimmed with fabric in a contrasting stripe.*

TOP CENTER *This small window, beneath which there is some rather attractive paneling, is an ideal candidate for an original piece of material. Suspended by rings from an iron pole set above the window, the fabric is caught back high enough so as not to detract from the overall shape.*

FAR LEFT (top, bottom) *This stagecoach shade is unlined but bordered with a contrasting fabric. The wide strips that support the shade break up the window and culminate in two large bows.*

41

Shades also work very well at small windows. They can be raised easily, which means that they do not obscure the available light. Roller shades, by virtue of their simple lines, are probably the best choice for small windows. A correctly proportioned Roman shade is also suitable, but the full sweep of an Austrian or balloon shade is usually overwhelming for a small window. Shades also provide an ideal opportunity for using a contrasting binding or border around the edge. Not only does this look dramatic, but it also defines the window and prevents it from seeming to float in the surrounding wall space. If you wish to maximize the window area, remember that shades can be hung outside as well as inside the window frame.

ABOVE, LEFT *Heavily textured Roman shades give a clean look to a boldly decorated room. The frame is painted white to contrast with the striped panels on the walls.*

CENTER, FAR LEFT (top) *An awkwardly shaped modern window, which is not only wider than it is tall, but also runs into an angled corner of the wall, needs very simple treatment. These curtains, plain in design apart from a subtle checked border, have been given a relatively deep, pleated heading that balances the border running around the entire curtain. The hem just touches the window sill, so that when the curtains are drawn, the window is at one with the wall.*

FAR LEFT (bottom) *These curtains are slipped over rods that are attached to the tops of the windows. The delicate braid that edges the curtains enhances the rural charm of the whole picture.*

Today, French windows and doors that open directly onto a balcony or into a garden are a delightful asset to a house or an apartment, bringing the outdoors inside in a charming and unique way. Depending on where in a room they are situated, they do not always need curtaining. Also, if the design is pleasing in itself, curtains of any type would be excessive. In this case, you could either leave them completely plain or hang an informal swag of sheer material or an antique textile over a pole that stretches across the top of the window.

If a French window does not stand alone but is, as so often happens, in the center of a pair of fixed windows, or if it matches other windows on another wall in the room, all the windows should be treated in the same fashion. They should be dressed with full-length draperies that are simple in concept and design. In addition, a single drapery is really preferable for a French window for practical reasons, and you should then try to tie in the design with the other more conventional windows

LEFT, BELOW, RIGHT This classically perfect set of French windows demands a classically perfect window treatment. Balloon shades were, in fact, originally designed for tall windows such as these. Here, they hang in perfect proportion to the rest of the room. The informally gathered shade above the French windows is set high enough so as not to impede the movement of the doors, while the two smaller windows on either side are dressed with smaller gathered shades. Both these smaller shades are balanced by an inner shade that is beautifully edged with an ebullient fringe.

French Windows and Doors

French doors are so called, not surprisingly, because of their extensive use in French houses, particularly in first-floor rooms and important second-floor rooms where full-height glazed doors were an essential part of the architectural plan. They grew in popularity across Europe during the late 18th and early 19th centuries, reflecting the leisured, pleasurable way of life pursued by many at that time and exemplifying the development of windows over the centuries as objects of beauty in their own right.

In the past, and particularly on the Continent, French windows, or doors, were often emphasized with a stiffened lambrequin or woven portière, which followed the lines of the window down the frame and often reached all the way to the floor. If your French windows stand alone, unencumbered by other windows, a contemporary version of one of these styles would be very striking. It might take the form of a shaped plywood frame that is painted, stenciled, or covered with fabric. Alternatively, a conventional stiffened valance could be made to extend farther down the sides of the window. Needless to say, any draperies hung beneath such dramatic frames should be simple in style and made in a relatively plain fabric.

in the room. Somewhat like a bay window, the French windows and the side windows can be unified by whatever you hang over the top. Indeed, if the frame around the door is a beautiful feature in itself, just drape a piece of eye-catching textile across a pole, either symmetrically or, even better, asymmetrically.

French windows may open outward or inward. If they open inward, the rod or pole must extend far enough beyond the edges of the window to allow the doors to open without obstruction. Should you need more

privacy, sheers can be used within the door frames or hung from the top of the frame. They can also be attached at both the top and bottom of the frame with a cased heading on adjustable narrow metal curtain rods. Loosely woven sheer fabrics such as muslin look better folded into loose pleats, or gathered slightly, than stretched taut across the frame.

Shades also work particularly well at French windows—with the possible exception of Austrian or balloon shades, whose fullness and slightly exaggerated style make them

BELOW LEFT *To draw in as much daylight as possible, the curtains at these narrow French doors are made from generous quantities of muslin, held back on each side by a cord. Above the curtains is an airy, fringed swag and cascades.*

BELOW, BOTTOM *A multidimensional approach for a pair of French doors is to treat each door separately with a narrow roller or Roman shade and to unite the two with a set of draperies on a pole. Here, the shades are in crewelwork, which is an unusual choice, and the outer draperies are sheer, partly to reveal the shades behind them.*

ABOVE, RIGHT *Glazed doors are not always set flush with the wall, and those with a deep recess need a treatment that will encompass the return. Here, a curved rail allows the draperies, with their neat pinch pleats, to completely obscure the architrave.*

LEFT *A pair of glazed doors is treated with full-length draperies made with grommets, which are slotted over a pole and tied back halfway down the door. Because the window is in a corner, a separate drapery serves the same function as a stationary panel, adding further importance to the whole scheme.*

largely unsuitable because they interfere with the mechanism of opening and shutting. They will also distract from the vertical lines of the window. Roman and roller shades are a much better proposition, particularly if they are used at French windows that are set within a large bank of other windows because the shades can be set at different heights in order to add variety and interest to the window shapes. The shades could be made from a solid-colored fabric and perhaps edged with a border to define them within the window space; if you prefer a patterned material, you will find that stripes or plaids are much more effective than allover or floral designs.

Often a French window is less a window and more a glazed door leading onto a balcony or terrace. If it stands alone, it can be dressed like a conventional French window, but if it is flanked by a pair of smaller windows, which do not extend to floor level, simply structured Venetian blinds may be the answer, with long blinds used for the door, short ones for the windows. When lowered, they will unify the windows in a manner that is not possible with curtains or draperies.

ABOVE, RIGHT When the French windows are particularly large, avoid large expanses of the same fabric. These full-size French windows are hung with alternate lengths of contrasting material. With so much interest in the fabric itself, there is no need for an elaborate heading.

LEFT, TOP At a pair of French windows that is not opened very often an alternative idea is simply to attach two lengths of fabric to the window frame using hooks, rings, and nails instead of brackets. One of the panels may then be tied back in order to let in air and light.

Bay and Bow Windows

Some people feel that a bay window is difficult to treat, but in fact, as long as each window within the bay is treated in a similar fashion, all is simplicity itself. This applies even if there is a relatively large area of wall between each window. The number of windows in a bay ranges from three to six or seven, and the curtains or draperies can either follow the angled shape or run across the bay to create a flat projection; this is often done in a modern-style house. A bay window also increases the levels of light and the sense of space in a room, so if you are lucky enough to have one, regard it as a bonus rather than an irritant.

If your bay window is fairly flat and there is room within the recess, a single drapery panel on either side of the area should suffice. Bay windows also often have an expanse of wall within the bay, in which case you should place two narrow panel draperies on either side to cover the wall along with a pair of functional draw draperies across the window itself. With a large surface area of glass, a single pair of draperies is too bulky and heavy for the window, as well as difficult to close. In this case, it would be much better to hang at least two panels between the separate windows and place the rods over the architraves.

You can unite the different windows within a bay by hanging sheer draperies over the whole window area, or alternatively by putting shades over each window and uniting them with a set of panel draperies at strategic points. For angled bays, which probably make up the majority

RIGHT, FAR RIGHT *This bay window, which has separate, red-and-white striped, full-length draperies at each of the windows, does not have a continuous valance running around the whole window. However, the overall effect of the window is unified by the inclusion of a very delicate shade, with a rather elaborate, decorative fringe that hangs at the center window. This shade serves to diffuse the light when the draperies are held in place during the day with simple tiebacks.*

of bay windows, you will need a cut-to-measure rod, which is widely available. You can either use angled rods, which follow the contours of the window, or, alternatively, continuous, curved rods attached to either the wall or the ceiling.

During the 18th and 19th centuries, bay windows were often headed with a heavy valance with draw draperies hanging below. Indeed, a bay is the one window on which some kind of continuous heading is almost essential, uniting the individual windows and the draperies. It should not be overly elaborate or concealed beneath an excess of frippery. The heading needs to be specially designed and possibly geometrically angled. A particularly dramatic effect can be achieved by fixing a wooden cornice board that has been cut in a continuous curve to follow the bay around. This would transform the window from an area of squared angles to one of flowing curves.

Rooms with bay windows are not always well proportioned, which means that the bay appears at odds with the rest of the room, further affecting its overall shape. If this is the case, you could design the draperies as if they were part of a theatrical stage, cutting straight across

LEFT *In this simple contemporary solution to the perennial bay problem, a three-bay window has been hung with deep Roman shades, one at each bay, and a pair of heavier, conventional curtains hung at the edges of the window. Both curtains and shades are in pale, off-gray tones, and the lined shades are thick enough to keep out nighttime drafts.*

ABOVE, LEFT, RIGHT *These draperies on a bay window in a period house are headed with deep smocking. Set beneath a continuous cornice, the carving of which resembles the smocked heading, the central draperies are caught together, while the outer draperies are held back with decorative pegs. The material of which the draperies are made is beautifully edged with tiny, subtly colored tassels.*

OPPOSITE *Resembling an oversized party dress, these draperies, with an elegant heading are ideal for a shallow bay window. The dramatic treatment is continued with the tiebacks, which are nearly at floor level and encourage the bottom of the draperies to sink gracefully to the floor.*

the opening so that the bay window is hidden when the draperies are closed. The area within the bay window could be separated still further from the rest of the room by furnishing it with comfortable chairs and a small table, which would give it a different function, perhaps as a writing alcove or a reading room.

Sometimes a bay is not the only window along the wall of a room. The bay window is often at the front of the house with another

smaller window nearby. However, both windows can be united with draperies that have the same heading or even a cornice or valance that runs across them both, including the alcove of the bay. This arrangement requires only the lightest of touches as far as the valance or cornice is concerned. In such a case, and for a single bay window where the

bay is particularly deep, you might like to consider installing a window seat. This would not only anchor the bay window in a confident manner but also suggest a feeling of leisure, especially if the seat were fitted with soft cushions made either in the same fabric as the draperies or at least in a material that complements them. You could pile some large

ABOVE *This bay is unified by using the black border material to make a separate knotted tassel to hang from the center of each window. While the draperies themselves are longer than usual, the knotted tassels extend down only to sill level.*

TOP RIGHT *In keeping with the rest of this pretty living room, billowing Roman shades in an almost sheer fabric are hung at each window.*

RIGHT *Curtains of heavy lace bordered with a deep band of contrasting color and texture at the base make a dramatic treatment for a tall bay.*

pillows on top of the seat to make the area in front of the bay window even more inviting.

Bow windows have always been admired and treated with much care, their pretty shape being a delightful sight from both inside and outside the house. When you are dressing a bow window, emphasize the shape of the window rather than disguise it. A curved rod hung with conventional draperies or even a softly curved shade would be a suitable solution. If you use a shade, do not be tempted to add any additional decoration or detail.

However, if you wish to decorate the shade, you should try to be as restrained as possible. Remember that a bow window is an attractive feature in itself and should be on display, rather than obscured beneath the ruffles of an overdressed shade.

Furthermore, a bow window and the space beneath it should always be regarded as part of the room in order to create a unified effect. This means that, as long as you have sufficient space available, you can install a seat or even a set of low, curved bookshelves that follow the line of the window.

LEFT *A bay window in a bedroom has been treated in a way that makes possible different drapery solutions by day and by night. During the day, sheer white shades are raised or lowered as required, while at night a pair of heavy cream curtains are pulled across the length of the bay for warmth and privacy.*

BELOW *In a more sophisticated version of the above, the curtains have been made to follow the lines of the window. If you are using shades and curtains in close conjunction with each other, the choice of textiles and patterns is obviously very important.*

Arched Windows

Arched windows can be dressed with a deep balloon shade in silk or other lightweight material, so that the curved edge of the shade echoes the curve of the window above. Keep the fabric light and voluminous and eschew ruffles along the bottom; silk, although expensive, is ideal. Other options include an unlined cotton chintz or even a heavy sheer.

Conventional drapery styles can also be used at arched windows. The draperies may be made with a relatively stylized heading, such as pinch or French pleats, which is attached directly to the window frame and follows the curve of the window. The draperies could then be tied back at the point on the window where the curve of the arch turns into the downward fall of the frame. However, bear in mind that such a design would really work only if the draperies were used as stationary panels and rarely, if ever, untied and allowed to fall. Another simple solution might be to hang the draperies from a very narrow rod, placed at the top of the straight sides of the window, in the style of café curtains, leaving the curved top to rise above, free of constraint.

Alternatively, a cornice board or valance could follow the curve of the window, being set above and beyond the window itself. Depending on the depth of the cornice, you could then hang draperies from a conventional rod beneath. If full draperies are not needed, sheer curtains could also hang from underneath a valance, a style that enhances the feeling of lightness induced by an arched window.

A window with a curved top is also the ideal place to try a swagged design whereby a relatively heavy piece of material is attached to the curve of the window and then caught back asymmetrically while a soft fiberglass curtain falls to the floor from underneath. An arched window can also be dressed attractively with light, louvered shutters, perhaps reaching up only as far as the straight sides of the window, which can be folded back during the day and closed at night.

ABOVE *An arched window is a thing of beauty and something to be admired rather than hidden. This spectacular example has been treated in exactly the right manner—left alone, and flanked by discreet wooden shutters.*

RIGHT *Rather than an attempt being made to follow the lines of these arched windows, simple curtains have been hung on a pole set slightly away from the window frame for nighttime use. They can be pulled right back to leave the windows uncluttered during the day.*

FAR RIGHT *A trio of fine 19th-century arched windows are set off by their original wooden shutters, which have been stripped back to the wood and waxed. No other ornament, or color , is required.*

Door Draperies

In Victorian times, draperies were often used to frame doors, and door draperies are still used today either to dramatically mark an entrance or simply to combat cold and drafts. In the latter case, fabrics such as velvet or silk are ideal because they are warm.

Door draperies can also correct the proportions of an ugly door. If the door is too small for the wall or there is an unattractive "dead" area between the architrave and the ceiling, a drapery with an interesting heading could be hung above the door. Alternatively, the drapery might be hung from underneath a decorative lambrequin, cut to run down either side of the doorway.

Should you want a door drapery on a drafty outside door, it is, of course, important to ensure that it does not impede the movement of the door. The usual solution is either to hang the drapery on the door itself, rather than on the frame, so that it opens and closes along with the door, or to hang it on a hinged rod that swings back against the wall when not in use.

ABOVE *A drapery is used instead of a door to separate two parts of a house. Tonal harmony is achieved by coordinating the colors of the drapery with the handpainted stripes on the wall.*

TOP RIGHT *A drapery over an exterior door has been attached to the door, but sits far enough away to allow the door to open freely.*

RIGHT *An ingenious solution for a door set into a narrow wall with little space to spare is to hang a deep shade, attached to the top of the door frame.*

FAR RIGHT *An otherwise severe environment is softened by a prettily patterned door drapery.*

LEFT *Only the most straightforward of curtain designs will succeed on a half-glazed door.*

FAR LEFT *In an apartment where one room leads directly into the next, a door drapery is a stylish way to divide the space.*

Room Dividers

Draperies make good room dividers and are particularly useful when one room has several different functions. Indeed, a pair of draperies could be used where a dividing wall has been partially knocked through, leaving a rectangular bridge or arch, especially if the resulting room looks too long. If the draperies can be seen from both sides, you should use the same fabric for both the curtain and lining, or at least two fabrics that complement each other and suit the room. They do not have to be of a similar weight, especially if the functions that take place in each part of the room are quite different—say for dining and sitting or for sleeping and living—but there should be some form of color and design coordination. For example, a warm damask could be paired with a scrunchy silk, while a floral chintz would go well with a lightweight striped cotton. These dividing draperies usually look best when secured with tiebacks or brackets, which will enhance the draperies' dramatic effect.

BELOW LEFT *In an all-white, light-filled bedroom, instead of a door separating the sleeping and dressing areas, there is a full pair of curtains, suspended from a circular, corona-like heading and attached with cord to the wall. This is a softer, more feminine alternative to a traditional door. The heading is a pretty design of appliquéd leaves.*

BELOW *In front of a staircase, a bright drapery, looped over a curtain rod, provides privacy and protection from drafts, as well as tying in decoratively with the colorful ceiling above.*

LEFT *A full-length drapery acts as a divider in a dressing room and gives privacy to a spare bed. The drapery is a delicately embroidered fabric with gold and brown stitching on a cream background; above the bed is a second complementary fabric, embroidered with elegant beasts.*

ABOVE *The curtains that divide this room into separate areas have been conceived as part of the overall dramatic and decorative treatment. Simply styled and made in heavy velvet, they are exactly the same color as the walls—a striking and unusual strong green—and the folds*

of the material highlight the red-backed painted wooden chairs on either side, as well as the paintings hung around them. They add depth to the room in a way that a door, or pair of doors— even if they had been painted in the same bright shade—could never have done.

Closet and Alcove Draperies

Draperies and curtains can be used in a host of imaginative ways: instead of glass or wooden doors over cabinets and other storage areas or simply to draw attention to the position of an alcove. One popular style is to thread gathered or pleated curtains onto narrow rods placed inside cabinet doors, behind chicken wire. When choosing a fabric for such a situation, there are some general points to bear in mind. If you are using patterned

RIGHT *A long run of hanging space is hidden by striped draperies—a far softer choice than an equivalent run of wooden doors.*

BELOW LEFT *Rich, deep-red curtains are used all around this bedroom—both to hide and to reveal.*

BELOW *Perfect for studio living, or a room with a dual purpose, heavy, rich-looking, floor-length draperies are a great way to conceal storage areas.*

BOTTOM LEFT *A simple closet is transformed into a glamorous storage space by a curtain that doubles as room divider.*

fabric, the size of the pattern is important. It should not, for example, be too large a print or too ill-defined, because when seen through the wire mesh it will look like just a colored blur. Stripes, small geometric prints, or even a solid-colored fabric with some texture would all work well.

Curtains made from a heavy fabric such as felt or velvet, headed in the style of a café curtain and slipped over a narrow rod, can be used to cover shelves in a home office. They are also ideal for covering open shelves in a kitchen or to conceal shelving in a bedroom or dressing room. Although people who rate practicality above decoration might demur,

fabric can also be used to completely disguise ugly heating apparatus such as radiator grilles.

Shades can also be used as an alternative to cupboard doors where space is limited. Pull-down roller or Roman shades over a series of shelves are, in fact, the perfect alternative to a row of built-in cabinets, which might otherwise look like vast expanses of wood and door handles. Many people actually prefer this solution, particularly in a narrow room or passage, because it eliminates the need for enough space to accommodate an open wardrobe door. Roller, Roman, or simply styled balloon shades will keep out dust and give a softer look than wooden doors.

Wall Draperies

It has long been fashionable, particularly in France, to substitute material for wallpaper, with the fabric usually permanently fixed to the walls. However, there is a persuasive argument for using material that can be detached easily, particularly for cleaning or when you are moving. In the past, wall hangings, such as tapestries or pieces of woven silk or wool, provided instant decoration as well as insulation and warmth. Indeed, by the 17th century, they were an important part of

the unified style of decoration that was so admired in England and on the Continent. In rural areas of Europe, the fashion continued for many years. Writing in the mid-19th century, the French novelist Honoré de Balzac describes how, on the feast of Corpus Christi, the wall hangings were taken down and hung outside the windows to decorate the façade and to suggest a festive atmosphere.

Voluptuous draperies, which were pieces of material hung in elaborate swags and then draped over cloth-hung walls, were also a popular fashion in England in the 18th and

19th centuries. The treatment was either pretty or overpowering, the latter often involving heavily draped damask wall hangings embellished with ponderous swags and fringed flounces. Imposing this may have been, but it is also rather excessive and suitable only if you favor a rich look for a dining room or a room used only on special occasions. A different approach, and one that is ideal if you prefer a simpler effect, might be to hang a wall-length drapery underneath a soft, straight valance in a contrasting color.

Other popular methods of decorating the walls include using a feather-light fabric such

OPPOSITE (above and below) *A heavy, quilted wall drapery in a high-ceilinged room serves two purposes. Not only is it a handsome decorative addition, but it also adds warmth and insulation to what could be a rather chilly space.*

LEFT *A collection of pictures and ornaments takes on a different aspect thanks to the backdrop of material on the wall.*

BELOW *A wall drapery that is also a headboard is a contemporary take on traditional canopied beds. This drapery is also an integral part of the room's decoration, made as it is from panels of material that echo both the bed linen and the edged linen mats that form a pattern around the bed.*

in between each point. Alternatively, the fabric can hang from a pole attached by brackets to the wall at either end. There is no need for the fabric to hang from ceiling to floor. In fact, when it is hung halfway or two-thirds of the way up the wall, it may actually serve to correct any flaws in proportion.

When the fabric hung against the walls is of the same design as the window draperies, it can be used to unify a room and give it a softer look. This treatment is quick and comparatively inexpensive to achieve, but it should be done as informally as possible so that the fabric looks as if it is not attached permanently to the walls. This informality is, after all, part of its overall charm.

Material can also be hung along the wall in separate panels or widths in an apronlike style and attached to the top of the wall with brackets or hung from rings on a pole. You can further define the widths of fabric by adding a border of braid or ribbon down each side and along the base. The draperies might be floor length or, in a room with a chain rail, finish level at this point.

as muslin or fine silk hung across a wall to provide a soft and inviting background for the contents of a room. This enticing effect can be employed successfully, for example, behind a bed or sofa set against the length of the wall. The fabric can be attached at various points along the wall so that it drops in shallow loops

In most rooms, the chairs and tables take their cue from the walls, and if you wish to emphasize the look on the walls, you should drape the same material, as long as it is fairly malleable, over selected chairs and sofas. This should be done in an artless fashion so that the fabric looks as if it has just been thrown there informally or simply secured at the back with a knot or a loosely tied bow.

You can also hang any striking length of fabric against a wall by means of decorative, fan-shaped clips fixed to a narrow pole. The fabric can then be moved around at will, as you would a painting. In the same way, an antique shawl may be hung on the wall simply to be admired rather than to serve a purpose.

Depending on what pattern or design of material you choose, hanging wall draperies is

ABOVE *In an angled bay, panels of sheer golden fabric hang from a black metal pole that follows the line of the architecture. Beneath, attached to the windows, are heavy white roller shades. This is a sophisticated way to add a decorative touch to an otherwise relatively austere style.*

LEFT *Not quite a tapestry, not quite a drapery, this material provides a perfect foil for a collection of art and other decorative objects.*

FAR LEFT (top) *This hall is transformed by covering the wall with a small piece of material that picks up the color of the chair.*

FAR LEFT (bottom) *When these draperies are drawn, the walls and windows of the entire room will look as if they are curtained. Variety is achieved by positioning smaller wall hangings at different points around the room.*

LEFT, FAR LEFT *Here, artfully positioned, tautly stretched wall draperies accentuate the rather inaccessible windows and fulfill a practical role.*

BELOW LEFT *This study corner is made both richer and quieter by hanging panels of thick material in contrasting colors across the wall.*

RIGHT *In an apartment with a dining area rather than a dining room, strips of natural-colored fabric, which are stapled at ceiling level and left to fall nonchalantly on the floor, provide instant drama and amusement.*

BELOW *Perfect for a rented room, these simple wall draperies, tied onto a wooden pole, can hide any number of structural imperfections.*

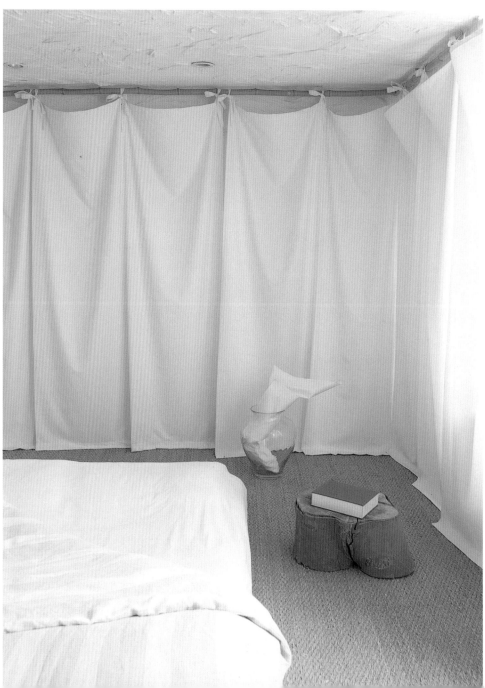

also one of the quickest and simplest ways of completely changing the style of a room without moving the furniture around. A scrolled and feathered damask, for example, immediately lends a period feel to a room, whereas strong plaids in bold colors or plain panels of fabric in citrus or other lollipoplike colors have a strong, modern look. Similarly, folds and drapes of fabric imply antique charm, while pieces of tautly stretched fabric suggest modernity.

Room Style

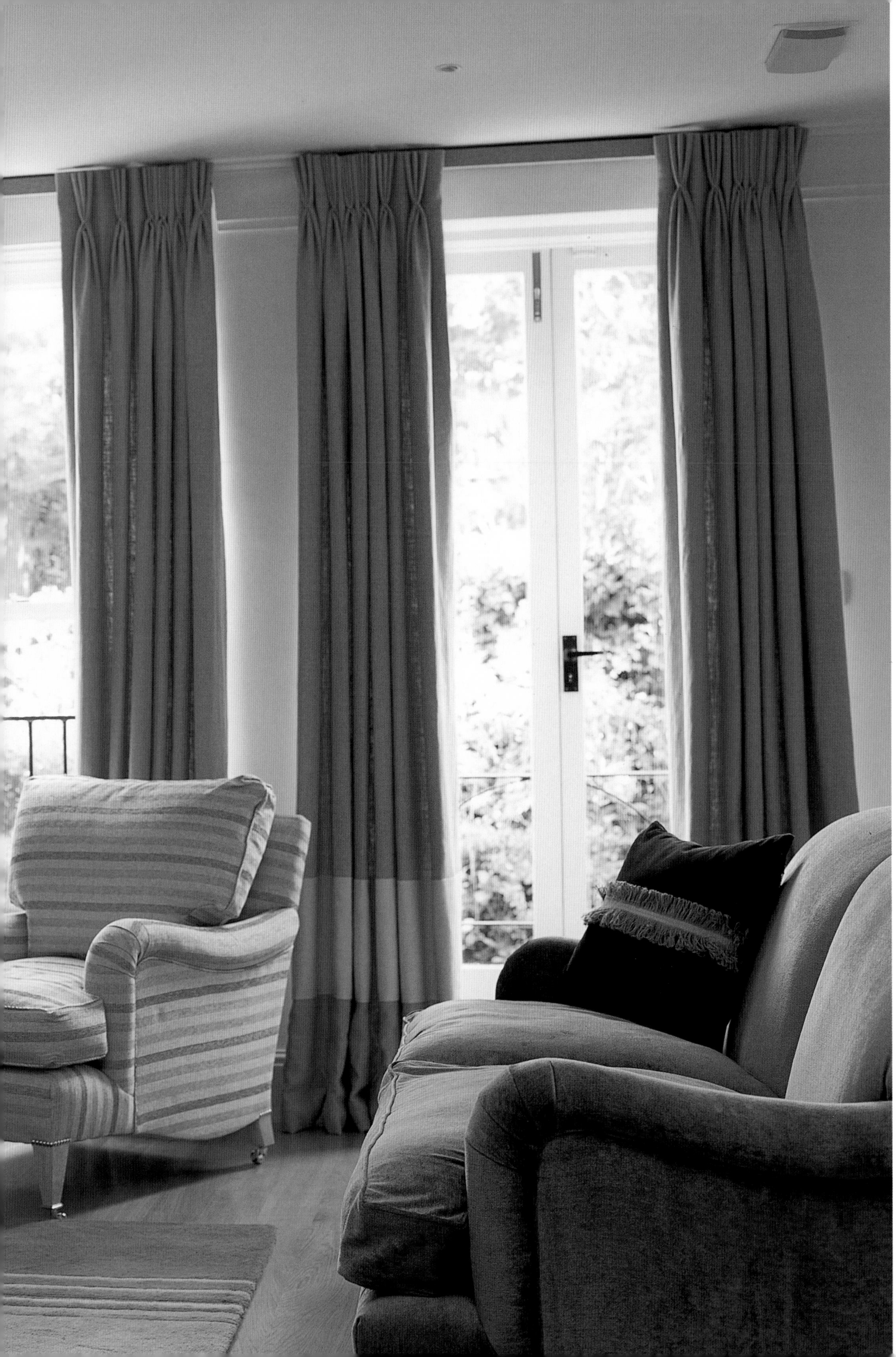

ROOM STYLE

Any window treatment should be appropriate to the architecture of the room and the house, and the stronger the architectural presence of a room, the more the draperies or curtains and any other furnishings should reflect that style. Although the draperies are important in themselves, they should also work well with all the other features of the room, from the floor covering to the color and finish of the ceiling. Rooms with different functions also lend themselves to disparate styles of window treatment made in various fabrics with diverse textures. Velvet, for example, has a deep pile and suggests warmth, whereas the geometric slats and reflective surface of plastic or metal Venetian blinds suggest cool efficiency. Many rooms now have several functions, which means that they take on a different air—not necessarily a more informal air, but one appropriate to the activities that take place there. So, the furniture, decoration, and furnishings of such a room should reflect these activities both practically and decoratively. By far the most important consideration when planning a room scheme, however, is that the style should suit you personally, both aesthetically and in terms of how you use the room.

ABOVE *A bedroom window is hung with a Roman shade for insulation beneath a drapery that softens the lines of window and shade.*

LEFT *This window covering exudes as much confidence as the rest of the interior design.*

ABOVE *Any window treatment in a bedroom must be both practical and aesthetic. Here, full-length lightweight draperies, in a red checked design that echoes the colors of the printed quilt, are simply hung, caught by a tieback, in front of a pair of French doors leading to the garden.*

ABOVE *Clean, modern lines require equally simple, pared-down draperies. Here, the heading of these unlined draperies made in a plain fabric is concealed behind a wooden cornice board that links the window to other wooden features, such as the paneled door, in the rest of the room.*

Living Rooms

A living room can serve various functions. It may be a formal room, used mainly for entertaining—what used to be called (and in some places still is called) a drawing room. Or it can be the place where the family spends most time when relaxing at home. But whatever you call it, this room has—except in the most formal of situations—a much more relaxed, informal feel than in earlier times, and this should be considered when planning the window treatments.

So, before choosing a style for a living room, it is important to ask yourself when you plan to use the room, for what purposes and activities, and at what times during the day. The answers to these questions should influence the style and type of window treatment you choose.

If your living room is more for the family than for entertaining, then classically formal draperies are not de rigueur, and would probably be inappropriate. If the room is used for combined leisure pursuits, then the decoration, including the draperies, should convey an air of easy relaxation. For example, rich drapery styles made in damask or brocade would look wrong if the rest of the room is furnished in a more utilitarian style. Linen and cotton fabrics, on the other hand, have an air of informality. They are also more practical, being easier to keep clean than more elaborate textiles. This is an important consideration in

RIGHT, TOP LEFT, CENTER LEFT *This living room has a timeless quality and will look as good in fifty years as it does today. Each element is in harmony with the others, including the draperies, which flow naturally from behind the wooden cornice boards. These boards seem to merge into the walls, almost like a continuous cornice.*

LEFT *In another corner of the same living room, the continuous cornice boards are clearly seen running around the perimeter of the walls.*

a room that will probably be used more than any other in the house. Living room draperies should also add warmth in winter and allow in the maximum amount of light in summer. Simplicity is the best approach. You will find designs that are easy to live with include irregular floral patterns, wide stripes, and solid colors in a distinctive weave.

Once all self-respecting drawing rooms had both summer and winter draperies, so that heavier draperies for cold evenings could be replaced with lighter, often flowered, chintzes in the summer. Today, daily life and available time—even available money—do not usually allow for such refinements of taste, but perhaps an argument can be made for

ABOVE In an uncompromisingly contemporary interior, the curtains should be considered as part of the architectural concept, along with every other element in the design. Indeed, their texture must work and contrast favorably with any stone, glass, and wood incorporated in the scheme. Designed to hang at a large picture window that looks onto a courtyard, this curtain treatment is simple, yet relatively luxurious, due in part to the large quantity of fabric used.

RIGHT, FAR RIGHT In this comfortable living room, simple white curtains are rescued from the conventional with bands of contrasting color, one narrow and one broad, the upper band creating the impression of a deep valance. The curtains are attached to the wire with thin white strips of cord tied to narrow rings.

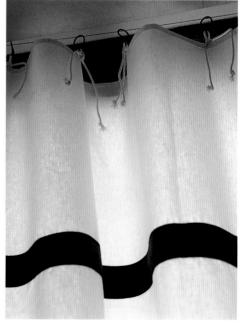

draperies that can be minimized and maximized to provide the same effect. For example, bold panel draperies might be accompanied by a shade, to be used in the winter, with the draperies hanging alone in the summer. Alternatively, panels hung over a self-patterned muslin or other sheer curtain might be removed for the summer, leaving the transparent curtain under a swagged valance.

TOP RIGHT *In a room filled with ornamental and decorative items, the full-length curtains have deliberately been kept simple and unfussy.*

ABOVE, RIGHT *The pale curtains at this unusually tall window are anchored by the band of decorative braid set in at chair height.*

CENTER RIGHT, FAR RIGHT *These Roman shades are adorned with decorative red stripes.*

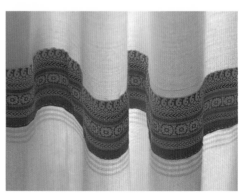

Although both roller shades and, to a certain extent, Venetian blinds were widely used in Victorian drawing rooms, they seem to be less popular today. But they can, in fact, be extremely effective if the room is small but formal. If, however, you prefer a softer look than that given by roller shades or Venetian blinds, Roman shades work well, their rectangular lines, balanced by soft, horizontal pleats, looking just right at single windows. The lines of the shade and the window may be accentuated further by a vertical border.

If the room will be used as a drawing room, the windows should be dressed with style and confidence, and possibly quite grand in concept. Extravagant draperies probably reached a peak of perfection in the 18th and early 19th centuries and can look just as good today if they are tempered with an element of simplicity. This simplicity is the most important aspect of the new thinking in design, affecting almost every part of the decorative scheme. Where possible, however, a drawing room should make some sort of statement, even if the statement consists of something as simple as painting the surrounding window frame in a strong, contrasting color.

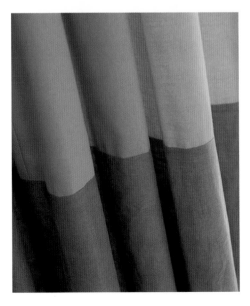

Traditionally, formal draperies should follow a certain pattern even when treated fairly simply. They should nearly always be floor length with a striking heading or valance caught or held back in some way. They will not be successful in rooms with the wrong proportions or with very low ceilings, even if the windows would respond to floor-length draperies. When planning formal draperies, you should treat the rest of the room equally formally: hammocks, beaded floor cushions, and ethnic throws should be saved for other rooms in the house. The furniture should also suit the dimensions of the room and be arranged in an orderly way.

FAR LEFT, BOTTOM LEFT *Well-proportioned windows can be hung with relatively simple draperies. The wide stripes of color in the floor, furnishings, and curtains provide an air of calm.*

LEFT, CENTER LEFT *A collector's room, full of diverse objects, often has enough to stimulate the eyes of the onlooker, so the windows are discreetly covered. Here, the Roman shades set within the architrave are functional as well as subtle.*

BELOW *In contrast to the eclectic choice of furniture in this living room, the treatment of the two windows is simple to a fault, with only a discreet design element introduced in the heading of each pair of curtains.*

Formal draperies should be full and made in a material chosen for its weight and texture as much as for its design. Damasks, brocades, velvets, and heavy linen all work well, as do chintzes, which should be interlined as well as lined to give them the necessary weight. The choice of pattern should be influenced both by the intended proportions of the draperies and by the height of the room.

ABOVE LEFT *A first-floor living room of simple severity has full-length draperies of white linen, caught high and falling in an elegant sweep.*

ABOVE *Formal drapery, no matter how simple its headings, should always be designed in proportion to the rest of the room. These warm gold and terracotta curtains not only emphasize the warm yellow walls, but also highlight the painted and gilded decorative panel between the windows.*

LEFT *Since the window area in this room extends along one wall and around a corner, the decision has been taken to keep the draperies themselves as restrained as possible, with only the simplest of headings, hung from a narrow black pole.*

RIGHT *Formal period pieces—an Empire sofa and chairs—are accentuated by draperies that are deliberately informal in design: wide checks, in the same color as the upholstery, are hung loosely from a wide wooden pole.*

Dining Rooms

A dining area may form part of the kitchen or living room or, as in the past, be a separate room devoted solely to entertaining and eating. Obviously, before deciding what style of draperies to have, you should think about what type of dining room you would like.

Some homes still require a formal dining room. If this applies to your home, avoid a halfhearted approach to decoration. Draperies in a dining room should make a strong, even dramatic, statement. What is a meal, after all, if not a production? The dramatic style suits almost any shape of dining room and window, except perhaps a room with a low ceiling and small windows. The effect should, however, be subtle: drama does not mean "over the top," but a bold statement delivered with panache. Such dramatic style could also incorporate an element of surprise, perhaps in the use of color or in unexpected details.

If your dining room is used only at night, window dressings can be even more dramatic, particularly if you prefer to eat by candlelight, which is the most effective way of setting the dining scene. For example, the draperies might fall in folds on the floor. If you opt for this look, the draperies should be panel draperies and never drawn. Artfully arranged, and overlong, such draperies would not have the same artistic appeal if pulled together every night. Alternatively, panel draperies may be joined at the top and held back by metal or wooden brackets. If the room is used at night, panel draperies are best paired with draw draperies, shutters, or shades.

The color and type of fabric for draperies in a room used only in the evening should be different from those in one used all day long. Colors that would appear "washed out" are not the best choice. Textiles that absorb too

ABOVE *In a small country dining room, furnished and decorated in a charming and simple way, the draperies, set inside the window recess, are designed to blend with the rest of the room in both color and style.*

LEFT *This dining room is used both as an eating place and as a background for the display of decorative objects and furniture. In keeping with the room's informal splendor, the window treatment consists of a balloon blind in a delicate printed material. A style that is notoriously difficult to achieve successfully, this example has just the right degree of panache, with both the proportions and the scale of the design working well with the window and the other elements in the room.*

much light are not suitable either, although if the fabric has a deep pile, as velvet does, it can introduce a sense of luxury to the room. On the whole, pale, light-reflecting chintzes do not work as well as bold, strongly patterned ones, while soft, semiopaque fabrics are less effective than well-defined materials.

For many people, however, a separate dining room is not an option, either from choice or necessity. Lack of space and a more informal way of life mean that many of us prefer to have a dining area within the kitchen or as part of a larger living area. The essential requirements, however, remain the same. In a combined kitchen and dining room, colors should be warm and relaxed, the light diffused and soft. Window treatments, including draperies, should be designed to allow in as

ABOVE *This kitchen and dining room in rural France is utterly comfortable and welcoming. Everything is geared to relaxation and the outdoor life—French doors open directly into the garden— and the curtains reflect this, made as they are from fresh red gingham checks, a design always associated with country life; the warm color is picked up in the rug under the table. The curtains are hung on a pole that extends beyond the window, allowing the doors to open freely.*

much light as possible in the day, yet full enough to provide a cozy feeling at night.

The choice of fabric is as important for informal dining rooms as it is for formal ones. Think carefully before using a floral design unless it is quite structured, because it can clash not only with the food but also with the table setting. Your choice should be neither too bold nor too subtle. Solid colors work well, perhaps with a contrasting border, braid, or fringe around the edges, while geometric designs fight with neither food nor table.

Floor-length Venetian blinds can also be effective, filtering the light and enabling you to create different lighting effects throughout the day. Another option, which is ideal when the room functions as a kitchen and dining room, is to use the same material in both areas but as roller or Roman shades at the kitchen windows and draperies in the dining area.

ABOVE *In a loft space divided into separate living areas, unity is achieved by curtaining the entire window wall in white, sheer, floor-length fabric.*

ABOVE LEFT *White sheer curtains beaded by a deep valance in the same fabric is the only window treatment needed in this serene, no-color room.*

LEFT, TOP *The relative starkness of this cool dining room is softened by the full draperies that run the length of the wall; the curtain rod has been incorporated into the decorative scheme.*

FAR LEFT *In a graphic dining area, an unusual high and long window is hung with a series of mono-toned roller shades that become, when drawn, extensions of the wall.*

RIGHT *A breathtaking view of the city skyline requires nothing more complicated than a full drapery in a color that will not detract from the sight of the wonders beyond.*

CENTER *Furniture and furnishings in this dining room come together in a design reminiscent of the painter Mondrian. Against a strong yellow background, the window, the picture frames, and even the central light harmonize with the design of the curtains, where different widths of color form a deep border on a canvas of pale cream.*

BELOW, BELOW RIGHT *The impact of this window is maximized by extending the draperies beyond the architrave. The almost imperceptible design of the slightly shimmering material creates a sense of peace and calm.*

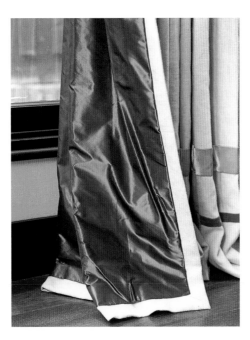

LEFT *A rich surprise is found on the reverse of these restrained, sophisticated draperies: they are lined in lustrous green taffeta. Such an original touch adds yet another subtle element of color and texture to this striking room (shown center).*

BELOW LEFT *A raised dining area with rather elegant furniture takes center stage in an uncluttered room. A simple interior design statement of this kind demands an unobtrusive, functional window treatment.*

BELOW *An elaborate cornice acts as a frame for a wide shade that completely straddles the window in a small dining room. The shade is sewn together in such a clever way that the seams follow the vertical lines of the window frame more or less exactly.*

Kitchens

Over the years the whole concept of the kitchen has changed. Not so long ago, even curtains—let alone full-length draperies—would have been out of keeping with the rather hard, sterilized look of the kitchens of the day. But today, since so many people spend more time in the kitchen, often using it as a living room as well as a dining room, curtains add an air of comfort. Yet, however cozy a kitchen is, remember that it is for the preparation of food. Hygiene and safety are of paramount importance, and since the fabric used for curtains or shades will get extremely dirty and greasy—which will be clear to anyone who has ever tried to clean the filter of a range hood—you should choose a fabric that can be easily cleaned.

ABOVE, TOP RIGHT *These full-length draperies in a kitchen-cum-living-room are designed so that they do not detract from inevitable kitchen clutter; they run efficiently on a traverse rod.*

RIGHT, CENTER RIGHT, FAR RIGHT *A full-length drapery is combined with a translucent roller shade and adorned with a wide band of fabric that almost reaches the level of the table.*

When deciding on a style of curtain for the kitchen, remember how busy a place it is. In consequence, it is ill-advised to have very elaborate draperies. They would simply look out of place and clash with everything else. Any design you choose should be simple and relatively clean in line. Café curtains, for example, are an ideal choice, allowing you both light and privacy.

Shades or blinds are perfect for the windows above the sink or the drain board. Contained and businesslike, they can look both attractive and welcoming. However, some shades, even if treated, are quite difficult to keep clean. If that bothers you, Venetian blinds in wood, metal, or plastic, which can easily be wiped clean, would make a much better choice for a kitchen.

LEFT *In much of Europe, particularly in the French and Italian countryside, it is customary in kitchens to use curtains instead of wooden doors to conceal shelves under counters. Always decorative, curtains in printed cotton add color and pattern to a kitchen and have the extra advantages of being cheap, easy to change, and easy to launder.*

RIGHT *A wooden shade placed outside eliminates the need for anything more elaborate than simple, unlined curtains, which are made in a blue-and-white checked fabric.*

BELOW, FAR RIGHT *All is not as it seems with this window treatment. The Roman shades are flush with the window, while the decorative headings, which have horizontally striped edges, are slotted onto separate wrought-iron rods.*

OPPOSITE (right) *Probably the most efficient window treatment in a kitchen, especially one with more than one window, are shades that tuck neatly away, far from grease and dirt. These translucent shades are set into the architraves, close against the windows, giving maximum light and space in what is a relatively small area.*

Bedrooms

Like every other room in the modern home, the bedroom has altered its function—and the way in which it is perceived. It is no longer used just for sleeping but often for watching television or working. But in every day there comes a time when it should be a place of rest, and the window treatment should reflect this.

Not all bedrooms are well proportioned. Indeed, more than any other room, bedrooms are often conjured from strangely shaped spaces such as attics and other areas under the eaves. Unified designs often work best in these badly proportioned rooms, with the same colors and tones used on the walls, windows, and bed to draw attention away from the conflicting angles and corners. Coziness, not

ABOVE, TOP LEFT *An ornate piece of textile is shown at its best when caught up on either side in order to emphasize the central motif. The walls are also decorated with an intricately patterned paper that contributes to the air of wealthy indolence that fills the bedroom.*

ABOVE LEFT *These tieback curtains are slipped over a pole and fastened at the center. A simple shade screens the light.*

grandeur, is the desired effect. Your choice of fabric is also very important: it should provide insulation and keep out the light. The curtains should also be lined and possibly interlined. If you choose a lightweight, pale-coloured fabric for the curtains, consider using blinds underneath, either conventional blinds or specially treated, blackout blinds, in order to reduce the levels of light at night.

Chintz is traditionally used in the bedroom and can look its prettiest and most effective there. English chintzes have been renowned since the 18th century and in and out of fashion ever since. Indeed, Elsie de Wolfe, the well-known American interior decorator, used chintzes in the early 20th century against a background of disapproval. The best new chintzes are designed with a

ABOVE *In the 17th and 18th centuries, the same material as that used for the draperies was often used to cover much of the furniture—and in the 21st century, in confident hands, such a treatment can still be effective. In this bedroom, the full-size couch and the draperies have been executed in the same fabric design, while the four-poster bed is in a complementary pattern. The informal curtain heading is echoed in the couch colors, and the woodwork is painted in harmonious tone.*

In the past, bedroom walls were often furnished with draperies that not only kept the bedroom a little warmer but also unified the overall look. They were either detachable or permanently attached to the walls. If fabric is hung on the bedroom walls, you might like to add an edging along the top and bottom, as well as along the sides, where the walls meet. The best option is to use piping made from the fabric on the walls or, more interestingly, in a color contrasting with that of the wall fabric, perhaps with the same choice of edging for the draperies themselves.

Wall draperies might seem excessive, but it is important to remember that fabrics and

subtlety that makes them potential heirlooms. Recolored and revitalized, these chintzes work very well in both traditional and modern settings. The French equivalent of English chintz is the *toile de Jouy*. These charming, single-color cotton prints are usually set against an off-white background and depict delightful pastoral and village scenes. The complexity of the designs is offset by the relatively simple color range, which is traditionally in various tones of red or blue but often in green, brown, or eggplant purple.

window treatments that would appear flamboyant in another room can look quite at home in a bedroom. For example, silk taffeta in bright colors, figured brocades, lengths of Indian sari fabric, or even Pollyanna-style ginghams all look wonderful in a bedroom. Decorative trimmings can also be used to add interest, so long as they are handled with a light touch. Indeed, multicolored braids and ribbons for edging and tying back will add drama to swags and cascades.

Bedroom windows are also the perfect place to use plain lightweight materials, such as white or cream muslin, figured and embroidered lawn, voile, or silk. Full-length

ABOVE, LEFT *A stiffened valance turns into a deep ruffle that is bordered in deep blue, as are the edges of the checked draperies. The headboard is covered in the same checked fabric to create a harmonious effect.*

ABOVE LEFT, ABOVE CENTER *A loosely curtained wall leads directly to the draperies, which are made of the same fabric as the wall curtains with the addition of a striped border; all the draperies are caught back with a bracket.*

FAR LEFT *Because this bed is placed in front of the window, the draperies are designed to look as much like bed hangings as window draperies.*

RIGHT, BELOW RIGHT *This unusual but highly effective valance treatment is made by using the undulating, wavelike pattern of the fabric horizontally rather than vertically, as on the drapery below. The whole effect is one of neat precision and sophistication.*

BELOW, BOTTOM RIGHT *Here, a false valance, adorned with a thick fringe, is attached to the draperies rather than to the pole above. This is a sensible choice of window treatment for a dark bedroom because it allows maximum levels of light into the room.*

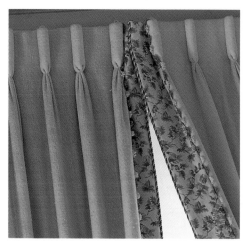

curtains or draperies made from an abundance of sheer fabric can also look extremely luxurious and feminine without being fussy. Sheer fabrics can, of course, be used for glass curtains; or they can also be used as draw draperies over a roller or Roman shade and topped by a valance.

Poles, whether they are made from metal or wood, painted or unpainted, also work well in a bedroom, particularly when they have lightweight finials. They provide decoration without being overbearing. A piece of material draped casually over a pole is always an effective treatment.

ABOVE, TOP LEFT *A bed in the center of the room and a bay window with a view of the garden are emphasized by these classic draperies with their simple pleated heading and border of suitably exotic contrasting fabric. The draperies fall open in an informal, even casual, manner at strategic points around the bay window, which gives the room an intimate atmosphere.*

Bed Furnishings

Bedroom window treatments should not be thought of in isolation. The bed, whether it is covered with a duvet, bedspread, or quilt, is an integral part of the furnishing scheme. This is even more true if it has bed hangings, which have gained in popularity recently. Through-out history the bedroom has been a place of privacy and comfort, as well as a means of demonstrating status, wealth, and power. More money was lavished on the bed

ABOVE, LEFT, RIGHT *This half-tester canopy projects from the wall behind the bed. The drapery against the wall and the pair of lined draperies that hang from the gilded cornice are made in the same two-toned, patterned fabric. The bed itself requires nothing more than a covering of crisp white sheets and some white linen pillows. The curtains at the window are simple in comparison with the bed treatment, while the fabric from which they are made matches the underside of the bed canopy.*

BOTTOM LEFT Another subtle approach, based on the idea of the traditional half-tester, has been interpreted by draping a simple pair of curtains from iron poles; the curtains frame a striking bust, set into a deep niche in the wall behind.

BELOW, BOTTOM RIGHT Today—unless your bed is antique and rather ornamental in design—less is often more in terms of bed furnishings. The discreet charm of this bed is shown in the manner in which the diaphanous fabric

behind the bed is draped from a central corona, and the fact that the blue-and-white upholstered headboard is designed to complement the hanging rather than imitate it. The bed pillows are a combination of the old and the new.

hangings than on any other accessories or piece of furniture. Much as they did with window draperies, the Georgians elevated bed hangings and draperies to a fine art, and the Victorians also considered an undraped bed to be bare and unfinished.

You may not like bed hangings, but they certainly add focus to the bed, which is particularly valuable when you consider that modern beds are lower than they were in the past. Dressing the bed can be done in a variety of ways, from the simple to the elaborate. It is

relatively easy to emulate the "state bed" look of the box beds of the past by cutting a cover to fit the size of the bed exactly and allowing it to fall to the floor without pleats or folds. If you have sufficient space, the bed draperies, made in the same fabric, can be headed with a straight valance which is in proportion to the depth of the bedcover. Heavy woven fabrics (those with a pattern that is woven rather than printed), such as tapestry or damask, are the best choice. To achieve the same effect in a small room, the bed could be pushed sideways into an alcove so that the walls create a box. A brass or wooden pole can then run across the alcove to support draw draperies.

In 17th and 18th-century bedrooms, the bed and window draperies often matched exactly. Even the cornice or valance of a four-poster bed exactly echoed the cornice or valance at the window. Today, this is usually seen as excessively elaborate, except in the most traditional of bedrooms, and, in fact, if the window draperies are particularly complex, very simple bed hangings are the only choice, and vice versa. However, if you decide to hang draperies around the bed, it is important that they reflect the overall scheme of the bedroom in some way. The window and bed draperies do not have to match, but the eye cannot help moving from the bed to the window and back

LEFT *In contrast to the polished terracotta floor, everything else in this room is white—from the heavy white draperies on the white-painted wooden bed to the white bed linen, window curtains, and even the upholstered chair.*

RIGHT *An antique four-poster bed has been upholstered and draped in formal and traditional manner, complete with fitted canopy and full curtains, which encompass the bed.*

BELOW *Long sheer draperies fall from a gilded corona into heavy waves of fabric at floor level. Blue and white is the theme—from the edging of the bed hangings to the coverlet and the soft ruffle at the window.*

ABOVE LEFT *Fabric can be used in many different ways to dress a bed. This traditional iron bed—which, in a small bedroom, has been set along the wall—is draped with curtains in a style reminiscent of the 'lit à la polonaise' design of the 18th century. The hanging gives the bed an air of permanence that it might otherwise lack.*

LEFT *This contemporary interpretation of a traditional four-poster design consists of a set of white bed draperies simply hung from metal poles attached to the ceiling with cord. Instead of a headboard, a decorative print in gray and white tones has been attached to a piece of painted wood and hung some distance up the wall behind the bed.*

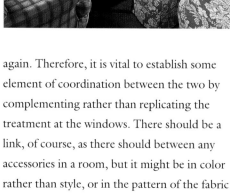

again. Therefore, it is vital to establish some element of coordination between the two by complementing rather than replicating the treatment at the windows. There should be a link, of course, as there should between any accessories in a room, but it might be in color rather than style, or in the pattern of the fabric rather than *passementerie*.

Toward the end of the 19th century, technical advances introduced tubular metal beds, which replaced wooden bedsteads with their traditionally heavy hangings. Instead of draperies designed to surround the bed, these new metal beds often had rods or narrow poles extending a few feet down from the top of the bed. Suspended from each pole was a small curtain made in a suitably light washable fabric that acted as a screen. Later, the advent of gas central heating eliminated the need for the heavy insulating hangings of earlier times, and for many years thereafter beds remained defiantly unadorned.

The last ten years have seen a new interest in the art and style of bed hangings, although, thankfully, the designs are not quite as complicated as they were in the past. The simplest of all are bed curtains that hang informally from poles fixed to the ceiling.

ABOVE *Against handpainted off-pink walls, the vertical lines of the white-painted, wooden beamed ceiling are echoed in the pink-striped bed curtains, the bed linen, and the upholstered bench.*

ABOVE LEFT, TOP LEFT *From the dramatic sweep of the bed hangings to the upholstered chairs and stools, everything in this room is in tones of pink—but each fabric has been chosen with such care and attention to scale and detail that the finished effect is one of pleasant harmony.*

RIGHT *A child's bedroom charmingly combines pink and white with a veillike sweep of fabric from top to toe of the bed. A decorative Chinese lantern hangs from the central point of the curtain.*

They can either fall gracefully to the floor or create a tentlike canopy. Such curtains can be unlined to achieve an even more informal effect. No material is too simple: muslin, cotton sheeting, lining silk, or undyed linen are all suitable. The curtains should be allowed to hang straight down or be tied back with a length of ribbon or braid.

Indeed, airy, almost frivolous, ways of dressing a bed are becoming increasingly fashionable. As in the 18th century, the bed may be set along against the length of the wall and a crown with curved iron rods used as a central point from which to drape curtains above and along the length of the whole bed. Known as a *lit à la polonaise*, it spawned many other fashionable versions. Alternatively, a corona, or crown, might be fixed over the head of the bed and dressed with fabric that drapes abundantly down on either side. Relatively simple to erect, a corona may be either antique or new. They are available in metal and sometimes in wood.

This look is, of course, highly feminine, but avoid confusing femininity with excessive fussiness or frilliness. If you do wish to indulge a liking for ruffles and flounces, either along the edges of the bed draperies or round the valance, make sure that there is enough simplicity in the other elements of the design to balance the frilly touches.

A draped bed does not, of course, have to be feminine. It can be hung with relatively formal draperies and treated in a masculine, almost severe manner. A half-tester or traditional four-poster bed would be more appropriate than any form of corona because rectangular forms are always more masculine than rounded ones. Half canopies were extremely popular during the 19th century and can be easily created today by attaching a false canopy to the wall behind the bed.

Bathrooms

The bathroom has changed in appearance over the last fifty years from a practical, almost utilitarian place to a delightful haven that often sports curtains or shades even if the bathroom window has frosted glass.

Many bathrooms need screening from the outside throughout the day, not just at night, and sheer curtains are ideal for this. They can be full length and cut like heavier curtains, half length like café curtains, or used with more traditional curtains or shutters. An unusual combination is to have one roller

ABOVE, TOP *Since bathroom fixtures and furniture take up so much space, simple curtains that can be easily cleaned are best. These are full and hang from a narrow metal pole attached inside the window frame.*

LEFT *The ultimate plastic curtain surrounds this bath, rather like a cocoon. The black-edged, circular wall mirror behind the bath turns the whole arrangement into a Mondrianesque design. The simplicity of the curtain treatment is ideal for the rather stark whiteness of the bathroom.*

shade made from stiffened material such as voile or gauze, fixed inside the window frame and another, which is only used at night for privacy and insulation, fixed outside it.

For added luxury, you can dress the bathtub. If the tub is against the wall, run a pole along its length and hang a curtain at the end farthest from the taps. For a bath with a shower, a fabric curtain can be used to hide the usually rather ugly plastic inner curtain. If the bathtub is freestanding, attach a corona to the ceiling above the tub and drape a pair of curtains so that they fall, tournament-tent fashion, down either side.

ABOVE *These striking, black-and-white shower curtains are hung from a fine wire, making them look as if they were suspended in space.*

TOP *The narrow entrance to a shower is made from louvered glass shutters, which maximize the available space in the bathroom.*

RIGHT *In this luxuriously comfortable bathroom, complete with a low-standing floor lamp, the windows are hung with a sheer yellow curtain that gives a sunny glow even on a gray day.*

ABOVE *A boudoir-like bathroom with its deep draperies and inner sheer curtains looks very cozy.*

TOP RIGHT *The light in this room is diffused by the translucent shades hung inside the architrave.*

CENTER RIGHT *A thick heavy drapery gives a shower room a voluptuous, opulent atmosphere.*

RIGHT *The curtain at this bathroom window has been made in a suitably piscatorial fabric.*

Curtains and shades bring warmth and style to a bathroom and a pleasing contrast to the inevitable shiny, reflective surfaces. As in the kitchen, the material used for any bathroom curtains should be lightweight and washable. Condensation, steam, heat, and damp all take their toll on fabrics. Cotton is undoubtedly the best material to use for bathroom curtains as it is easily washed and pleasant to the touch.

ABOVE, TOP *In a small bathroom, a striking and interesting window treatment must combine both practical and decorative virtues. This shade, which is made from strips of fabric woven into a simple lattice, is the perfect choice for a bathroom, allowing in sufficient light if raised while also guaranteeing a good degree of privacy whenever necessary.*

LEFT *Stretched tautly across the window, a printed sheer seems to float above the bath.*

SHADES, BLINDS, AND SHEERS

Shades and blinds play an important role in window design, excluding light and drafts when used with panel draperies or fiberglass curtains, as well as highlighting and completing a window treatment. Used alone at a window, a roller or Roman shade or a Venetian blind suggests a certain streamlined modernity. Shades come into their own in rooms such as the bathroom and kitchen or at windows where the amount of fabric needed for curtains would be impractical. Shades and blinds can also be used in other practical ways around the house, to conceal storage space where doors would be cumbersome or as informal room dividers.

The idea of a curtain or drapery that admits the light is hardly new, and sheer curtains of one description or another have been popular at various times for at least two hundred years. Today, in terms of fiber, finish, weight, color, and design, the choice of sheer fabrics is endless. There is a perfect sheer curtain for every purpose and situation, and lightweight see-through curtains are a useful decorative alternative to shades or draperies where light needs to be diffused or privacy maintained.

TOP LEFT *In this sunny bedroom, a lightweight fabric has been tossed over the curtain pole, giving an airy, almost casual effect.*

CENTER LEFT *A coarse-meshed fabric has been attached to the window frame and secured with a pole to provide a permanent screen.*

LEFT *A double layer of translucent roller shade and sheer, teamed with a traditional curtain in tones of white, gives a luxuriant effect in any room.*

RIGHT *Wooden louvered windows, the slats of which can be adjusted, allow for privacy in an informal room that also has angled windows.*

Roller Shades

Whereas most Roman shade material can be used unstiffened, the fabrics for roller shades should be chosen with special care. Many will need stiffening so that they can move easily around the roller. Although this process is not suitable for some fabrics, there has been much progress in stiffening techniques, and even some sheer fabrics and laces can be given enough body to hang successfully. Roller shades can be used to correct flaws in window proportion. For example, where there is a large expanse of glass, such as in very wide windows or in deep bays, a series of roller shades will break up the glazed area.

A word of caution is required if you plan to use a roller shade at a small window. The mechanical parts of a roller shade, namely the roller and the two end plates, require that the fabric start some way in from the ends of the roller. This means that you could have a light-revealing gap between the shade and the window frame. However, in rooms with

LEFT *These glass walls are dramatically treated with two large roller shades set at different levels.*

BELOW *A quirky take on the conventional, this heavy white roller shade has been designed back-to-front, as it were, with the workings—the cords and ties—displayed as part of the design.*

BELOW LEFT *A translucent white roller shade makes a decorative statement behind a low bench.*

BOTTOM LEFT *Oversized roller shades are used here to cover a sliding glass door.*

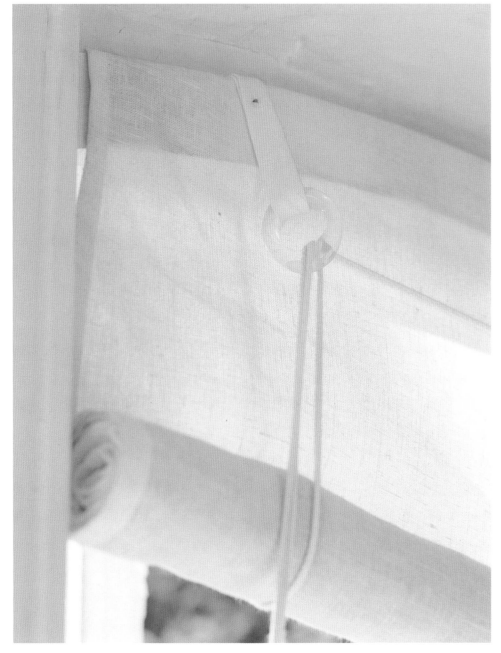

LEFT *In a bedroom where fabric is used in quantity, the window treatment has been kept low key: a roller shade in a fabric that matches the chair in front is teamed with sheer white curtains slotted onto a wooden pole.*

BELOW *A roller shade made of split cane has been hung from the top of the window in conjunction with half-shutters of wood that fold across the lower half of the window.*

BOTTOM *In a room decorated in minimalist fashion with polished boards and white walls, the windows have been hung with pure white, unadorned roller shades.*

sloping windows, roller shades are often the only answer, since they can be fixed at the bottom of the window so that the shade does not flap around when it is pulled down.

The choice of fabric for a roller shade needs careful consideration. Plain, striped, or plaid fabrics are more effective than those with abstract or floral patterns, which are likely to detract from the vertical lines of the shade. If you use a floral or figurative pattern, it is a good idea to anchor the shade visually by edging it with a border that picks out one of the colors in the design. The base of the shade could also be shaped to give it added interest.

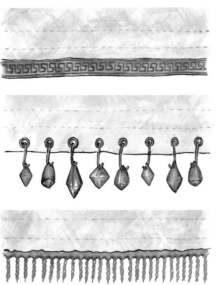

ABOVE *These translucent, rather insignificant roller shades are set against the windows to emphasize the classical proportions of the room. They are fastened at the bottom of the window rather than the top, but work on the same principle as any other roller shade.*

LEFT *Give a plain, ready-made shade an original, personal touch by adding a colorful border or edging. From top to bottom: a piece of braid, decorated with a Greek key design, is sewn along the bottom of the blind; brass grommets are used to hook on multicolored chandelier droplets that catch the light as they twirl; and some passementerie, in the form of fringing and gimp, is applied to the bottom of the shade.*

Roman Shades

Roman shades look more sophisticated, and often more formal, than the average roller shade. Although not seen in the past as often as balloon shades (presumably because they were not considered appropriate for grand windows), they were popular in England in the 18th century and earlier. They consist of a flat piece of fabric that pulls up into a series of wide pleats and, when let down, lies flat against the window. Roman shades look very striking set inside the window frame so that the surrounding architrave is exposed. Conversely, on a window that has shutters set into the casing, a Roman shade hung from the architrave allows both window frame and shutters to be seen when desired and gives extra insulation on cold winter evenings. It can also be used to soften the lines of a shuttered window.

The fabric used for making Roman shades does not usually need stiffening, although if they are hung in a bedroom or some other room where light needs to be excluded, it is important to line them just as you would draperies. This does not, of course, apply to a Roman shade made from sheer material, which is a sophisticated answer to diffusing light in a contemporary room in which long draperies would look inappropriate.

Roman shades not only emphasize the vertical plane of tall, narrow windows but can also provide a solution to the often difficult

BELOW LEFT, BOTTOM A room furnished in such a modest, classic style, with its collection of simple furniture and other soft furnishings, requires only the simplest of shapes at the window. Here, a Roman shade made in a rich, warm yellow fabric needs only the addition of triangular, handkerchieflike points as a decorative finishing touch along the bottom. This serves to complete the ordered symmetry that characterizes the rest of the living room.

RIGHT, BELOW This Roman shade is an especially good example of an updated traditional window treatment. Although the design of the material is classic, and the passementerie edging is even more so, the total effect is one of clean modernity. This effect is enhanced by the lines of the architrave which act as a handsome frame for this natural-looking textile picture.

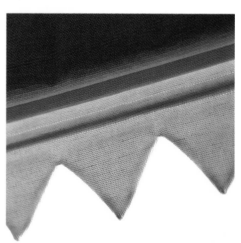

problem of dealing with a window that is curved at the top. Instead of being cut into a rectangle, the fabric can be shaped around a piece of board cut to fit the curve of the window.

Compared to curtains, Roman shades are fairly minimal in concept. A successful way to give them added character is to hang them from beneath a wooden cornice board. Shaped cornice boards, which are easily made with an electric jigsaw or coping saw, can be curved or shaped into ogees, arches, zigzags, or scallops. The board is then covered with

material—contrasting with that of the shade—or painted in a solid color and decorated with cutouts such as gold or silver stars, suns and moons, brass escutcheons, or other decorative trimmings. Another option is to decorate the board with a paper border; these are available in sheets from specialist suppliers.

Roman shades are fuller than roller shades and as a result look good at bay windows, particularly if they are set at different levels across the window. Indeed, as are roller shades, they are suitable for large windows and those that are composed of several panes.

LEFT, ABOVE *Within the usual parameters of their basic style, Roman shades can be designed to look more or less formal, according to the surroundings for which they are made. The large window in this very comfortable living room is hung with a Roman shade with shallow, horizontal pleats that draw up into what is almost a deep border.*

RIGHT, TOP *This large Roman shade is made from blue-gray silk—a particularly suitable choice of fabric, because the delicate texture of the material can be clearly seen when the light filters through it, bringing a calming atmosphere to the room. Using such a rich, luxurious material is also an ideal way of embellishing what is essentially a rather simple window treatment.*

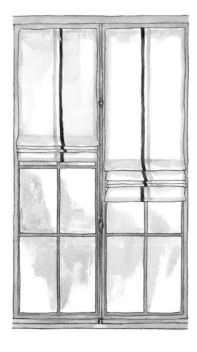

ABOVE *A pair of casement windows is dressed with two narrow Roman shades, the height of which is accentuated by the strong vertical lines of the fabric design.*

LEFT, TOP *When loose, woven fabrics are used for Roman shades, the result is obviously not as crisp as that achieved with a tight weave, but the loose pleats and the fold marks have an informal charm of their own.*

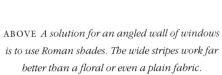

ABOVE *A solution for an angled wall of windows is to use Roman shades. The wide stripes work far better than a floral or even a plain fabric.*

TOP *A deep Roman shade that is as strong as the surrounding architecture suits a wall of windows.*

ABOVE RIGHT *This bedroom in the eaves has a softened version of a Roman shade, caught so that the softened pleats hang at an angle to the room.*

In fact, a row of shades made in a striking fabric will improve the visual impact of an overdominant expanse of glass. The effect might be accentuated further by making the shades in different widths and setting them at different heights across the window.

Like draperies, shades can be lined to cut out the light or for added stiffness. If, on the other hand, the shade is unlined the light shining through will give a slightly translucent look to the fabric and create a very pretty effect. Roman shades—or any type of shade, for that matter—are ideal for inaccessible windows. For example, if the window is set at an angle or follows the slope of a ceiling, shades made from a lightweight fabric and drawn over the window can be effective. The window will need an anchor point at the

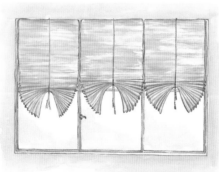

ABOVE *These loosely pleated shades are caught with a decorative center cord, so that the pleats fan down on each side. The different shades of cord are especially attractive.*

LEFT, TOP *With a simple Roman shade as a backdrop, the deep window sill of this paneled room makes a good display shelf. The window is not centrally placed, so a single-panel drapery on an iron pole is set some way out from the window to improve the proportions of the room.*

LEFT *A wide window in a country kitchen has been given a light-hearted treatment. The chosen fabric—a pattern of checks and stripes in a design and color echoed by the other soft furnishings—has been made into a Roman shade with a difference: instead of regular flat pleats, the shade is drawn up into a soft, more informal fold.*

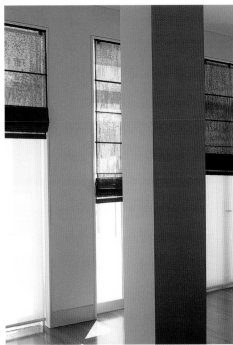

bottom to which the shade can be attached when drawn. They are easy to operate, which will enable you to bathe the room in light during the day and to view the sky at night.

Shades can, of course, be used in conjunction with draperies. Simplicity is the best approach. A neat effect is to edge the shade with a border of the drapery fabric, to unify the two disparate parts; or you might line the draperies in the fabric used for the shade.

ABOVE *A wide, shallow window looks much better with a finely shaped Roman shade than it would with a pair of bulky draperies.*

LEFT, ABOVE LEFT *Windows of different sizes running from floor to ceiling, some of which are obscured by pillars, need to suggest visual unity. These Roman shades, with their abstract design, both unify and add interest to the windows.*

Venetian Blinds

Venetian blinds were originally made from narrow slats of wood and first recorded in the 18th century, when they were known as *jalousies à la persienne*. In their first incarnation, Venetian blinds served the same purpose as slatted or pierced wooden shutters and screens in hot countries, allowing air through but deflecting the fierce heat of the sun. In our own century, the earliest Venetian blinds were made from wide slats of heavy plastic or metal and regarded as a clean, modern alternative to curtains or draperies.

RIGHT *This rather incongruous but effective window treatment combines a minimal white Venetian blind with a cornice board trimmed with traditional decorative fringe.*

BELOW RIGHT *This Venetian blind forms part of the decorative window treatment, rather than being regarded merely as a practical element. The unusual color of the blind is echoed both in the window frame itself and in the paneling below. When the blind is lowered, the whole window presents a seamless, united front.*

BELOW *Louvered white wooden shutters are a perfect choice for letting air and light into an open-plan summerhouse.*

Today, Venetian blinds are available in plastic, metal, or wood in a variety of colors as well as with slats in different widths. The slats are linked either with cord or with strips of fabric or webbing, perhaps made in a different color from that of the slats. Indeed, a strong color contrast can transform a blind; for example, contrasting stripes of color on plastic and metal blinds are very effective, whether they are deckchair wide or pinstripe narrow.

Venetian blinds can also be used as room dividers. If they are wooden—whether natural, stained, or painted—they could work well in a sunroom, while narrow-slatted blinds are ideal for bathrooms and kitchens.

ABOVE, TOP LEFT *These white louvered doors—which could be described as a pair of integral Venetian blinds—provide a useful solution for a window that looks out onto an inner courtyard or garden.*

LEFT, ABOVE LEFT *Wooden Venetian blinds, unpainted and raised by wide burlap tapes, add a feeling of rich warmth and a slightly more natural look to a modern room that has been decorated in a sophisticated manner.*

Sheers

The translucent quality of sheers and the way they diffuse daylight make them appealing for any shape of window. They can be used to good effect on their own or with heavier fabrics and look particularly dramatic when paired with a heavily textured wool or damask. One of the best designers of modern sheers, Celia Birtwell, sometimes hangs sheer curtains over, rather than under, a heavier curtain or drapery. The effect of the opaque material seen through a translucent fabric adds new interest to the simplest of window treatments.

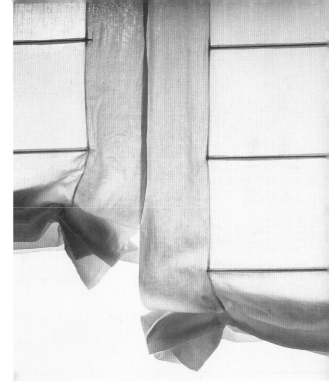

ABOVE, BELOW *These translucent linen shades, resembling large handkerchiefs, have an unstructured feel that counteracts the ordered, geometric design of the room in which they are set.*

LEFT *Sheer curtains are particularly effective in a bathroom, where they diffuse the light, give daytime privacy, and add an air of refined luxury.*

OPPOSITE (top left) *Dotted with tiny stars, the fragile-appearing fabric of this simple sheer curtain is emphasized by the heavy tasseled metal pole that is used to raise and lower it.*

OPPOSITE (below, top right) *A self-patterned sheer is particularly effective when used like a drapery made from much heavier material. These sheers are caught back beyond the architrave so that the glazed doors can easily be opened.*

There is a range of sheers in different weights and materials, from voile to gauze, often decorated with stars, flowers, and even stylized animals. Such ornamental sheers can be shown off by hanging them in front of a plain roller shade.

Sheers can be the epitome of luxury, and long, muslin curtains hung from a gold pole or underneath a gilded cornice board can look

ABOVE, BOTTOM RIGHT *A wide window is curtained with self-patterned sheers beaded with a deep ruffle made in the same fabric. When the curtains are released from the tiebacks, the ruffle has the air of a soft valance.*

TOP RIGHT, CENTER RIGHT *Beneath a cornice board, a double traverse rod holds a continuous sheer drapery and a heavier figured drapery made in a blue-gray fabric. Both draperies can run in unison on the one system.*

RIGHT *In an area that doubles as a living room and an exercise room, the laid-back sheer curtains are attached by extralong strips of material, softening what might otherwise be a rather cold, uninviting environment.*

very luxurious. So, too, can lace curtains, both hand- and machine-made, which are currently enjoying a revival. Panels of antique lace and good reproductions of them can also be found. If you are using antique lace, it is not essential that the panels at the same window match, but if they do not, avoid treating them as an exact pair. Instead, tie them back at different levels, or use one as a curtain and the other as a swag, draped across a pole.

Sheer curtains can also be very practical, being ideal for small windows, where they do not overwhelm. They can also be threaded over a rod at both top and bottom, which is especially useful in a bathroom or kitchen.

RIGHT, CENTER *The appeal of pristine, white curtains is timeless, and there is no necessity to dream up elaborate ways of hanging them. A heading of simple curtain rings, threaded over an old gilded pole, is counterbalanced by a deep hem.*

BELOW *When used as bed hangings, sheer fabrics have many advantages. Although giving an air of privacy and containment, they are neither stuffy nor heavy, and can be used—particularly if they are white—in conjunction with other textiles in the room without fear of overload.*

ABOVE *Although these sheer curtains could be regarded as rather extravagant and elaborate in any other setting, the delicate pastel colors of the fabric, as well as the intricate delicacy of the pattern, are seen at their best when the curtains are hung against the light.*

ABOVE *Sheer fabrics make excellent space dividers, in that they imply rather than pronounce, giving a feel of enclosure rather than cutting up the space; they are especially useful when demarcating a bathing or dressing area within a bedroom and when used with glass dividers, as illustrated here.*

ABOVE *In the context of interior decoration, sheer fabrics are multitalented and always open to suggestion. As well as providing curtains or bed hangings, they can also be used as wall coverings, giving a softness and subtlety of finish that neither paper nor conventional close-hung*

textiles can achieve. In this small bedroom, the sheer patterned fabric that has been hung at the window follows the line of the ceiling around and onto the adjoining wall. As well as giving unity to the decorative scheme, the use of a single fabric makes the room seem much larger.

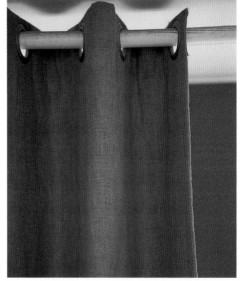

DETAILS

Draperies are a vitally important part of the design scheme in a room. They catch the eye immediately and are one of the first features that people comment on. A sofa, for example, has to look really terrible or absolutely wonderful before it is mentioned, but nearly everyone has an opinion on the draperies. Draperies, curtains, and shades can be greatly enhanced by adding decorative details, for it is the details that emphasize the design of the window treatment. The detail may be as simple as a braid, ribbon, binding, or a tassel, or as striking as an ornately carved pole with finials. Each detail you choose must be applied as carefully and neatly as possible, because the effect of the most beautifully made draperies will be ruined by an untidy fringe or a badly sewn tieback. When adding decorative details, do not confuse the idea of fine detail with fussy or fancy additions. The best details within any decorative scheme should simply emphasize the line of the draperies themselves. Not only must the details be beautiful in themselves, they should accentuate the beauty of the window treatment and the room.

TOP LEFT *A piece of fabric has been laid over the top of a curtain with apparent artlessness—but the textural contrast, the border, and the ribbon detail all draw attention to the window as a whole.*

CENTER LEFT *A contemporary take on the traditional curtain pole and rings is achieved by slotting an oversized metal pole through the metal-edged grommets of a heavy linen curtain.*

LEFT *The broad stripes of the material in this shade contrast with the natural weave. The shade is attached to the architrave by brass hooks.*

RIGHT *Against the dark wooden frame of the window, the curtain rings are tied with cords to a length of thin wire. Each piece of cord is knotted at the end in an informal manner that complements the simplicity of the curtain.*

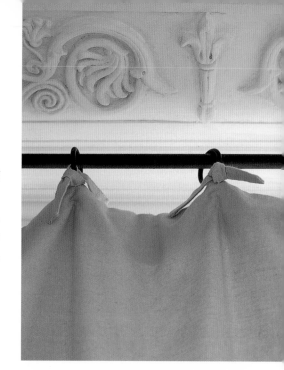

Rods, Poles, and Finials

Headed draperies with no cornice or valance can be hung on poles, but most other types of drapery should be hung from a conventional rod, usually made from either plastic or metal, and concealed behind a valance or cornice. An alternative to a decorative wooden cornice is a narrow piece of board covered in the same material as the draperies. The positioning of the rod when you are hanging your draperies is vital. It is either attached to the top of the architrave or, more probably, secured in the "dead" space between the architrave and the ceiling. It all depends on how elaborate and deep the drapery heading is.

A conventional rod is specifically designed to be functional. Beauty does not enter into the equation. These rods can be bought ready-made or custom-made to fit the dimensions of the window exactly. Cut-to-measure rods are available in curved styles to fit bow windows, or angled to go around corners. Double rods permit you to hang a pair of opaque draperies over sheers. Make sure to buy a good-quality rod, adequate for the weight of your draperies.

TOP LEFT *This drapery is designed for awkward corners and set onto a specially curved rod.*

CENTER LEFT (above) *One way to make a curtain from an antique sheet or hanging is to fold the hemmed side into a soft valance and attach the whole with decorative clips that slide over the rod.*

CENTER LEFT (below) *A smocked heading has a softer, more informal effect than a pleated one.*

LEFT *Widely spaced pinch pleats work well where there is no space for more elaborate heading styles.*

CENTER RIGHT *A wooden cornice is ornament enough for this simple drapery.*

RIGHT *A simple roller shade is covered by a drapery on a metal rod with decorative details.*

If the draperies are to draw (unlike stationary panels), you will need to use a traverse rod. In addition to conventional traverse rods, decorative styles are available; in these, the cords and sliders are concealed behind a hollow pole. A cheaper alternative, if the draperies are made from lightweight or sheer fabric, is to attach a drawing wand to the top inner corner of each panel. These are then used to open and close the draperies.

Whereas swags and cascades are sometimes seen as feminine, poles and finials have a masculine character and suit tailored draperies

LEFT *An elaborate and beautiful plaster ceiling cornice needs no more than a simple metal pole arrangement below it. The simplicity of the draperies also emphasizes, through contrast, the ornate complexity of the plaster design.*

BOTTOM LEFT *A quilted fabric, which has been trimmed to look as if it is reversed, is suspended from a metal pole by narrow contrasting rings.*

BELOW, BELOW LEFT *A brass pole and grommets, along with ornamental brass brackets, enhance the richness of the patterned fabric and the overall design of this comfortable dining room.*

and well-proportioned windows. Decorative rods are available in a variety of sizes, from narrow, brass café rods to thick wooden poles. They are useful, if not essential, when a drapery does not have an elaborate heading. Rods are also smarter than the spring-pressure curtain rods often used for bathroom and kitchen windows.

The most popular materials for both rods and finials are brass, iron, and other metals, as well as wood and resin, which can easily be molded into different designs. This means that finials can be as simple as a ball or as elaborate as a lion's head and mane. Finials are sometimes bought separately, and so it is important that they work well with the pole.

LEFT *These tieback curtains, permanently fixed at the center, are finished with a casing that runs through a pole with spearheaded finials.*

RIGHT, CENTER RIGHT *These draperies are suspended from a pole fixed just below the ceiling. They are unlined to the depth of the window, so they act somewhat like a sheer and pleasantly diffuse the light.*

BELOW *A peg board made to the same depth as the outer architrave is fixed above the window to provide an unusual support for the long loops of the curtain. The whole effect is simple but effective, reflecting the Shaker style.*

ABOVE *An inner sheer drapery and a chocolate-colored outer drapery are both headed in the same simple way to create a harmonious effect.*

LEFT *Tabs fix these draperies to a pole. A single tassel hangs prominently in the center and throws the draperies into sharp relief.*

RIGHT *These small white curtains, which hang beneath a bathroom sink, are tied with small bows to a thin rod. The intricate, lacelike edge along the bottom of the curtains brings an element of delicacy and femininity into a room that can often seem rather stark and utilitarian.*

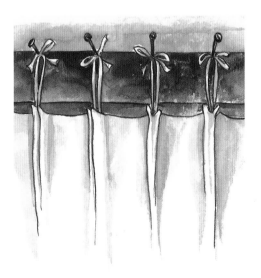

ABOVE *A lightweight curtain is attached to a pole by thin fabric strips sewn to the curtain and tied around the pole; this treatment would not work with a heavy, or lined, drapery.*

CENTER LEFT *Curtain clips, available in various sizes and finishes, give an informal effect.*

LEFT *In this treatment, the color and texture of both pole and metal slots are part of the design.*

FAR LEFT *Basic but interesting, this curtain is attached to the board by bows hanging from nails.*

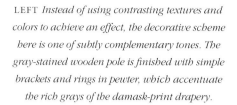

LEFT *Instead of using contrasting textures and colors to achieve an effect, the decorative scheme here is one of subtly complementary tones. The gray-stained wooden pole is finished with simple brackets and rings in pewter, which accentuate the rich grays of the damask-print drapery.*

RIGHT *A traditional wooden pole and rings are brought to life by the addition of a gleaming brass bracket. The rich dark color of the wood provides a beautiful contrast to the pale-colored draperies.*

BELOW LEFT *In a contemporary take on traditional curtain rings, a satin-brushed metal clip, fastened through what is virtually a large button hole, attaches the curtain to the rod.*

BELOW RIGHT *Antique French finials, brackets, and decorative rings provide a strong contrast to the unlined curtain beneath.*

FAR RIGHT *The addition of a decorative finial can give a successful finishing touch to any pole. From top to bottom: an openwork steel bracket; a silver-gilded wooden ball; a metal spiral; a gilded, neoclassic leaf; a brass spear; an ornate fleur-de-lys; a steel shepherd's crook; and a wooden furled leaf.*

BELOW *Finials available today range from styles popular in the 17th and 18th centuries to contemporary and even futuristic designs. Finials are made in a variety of materials including metal, wood, plaster, glass, and resin. From left to right: a gilded spear head; a turned wooden ball; a gilded leaf; a wooden acorn; a steel fleur-de-lys; and a turned, gilded globe.*

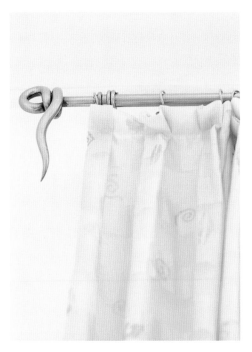

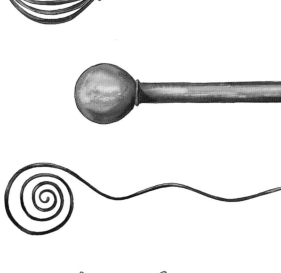

ABOVE *If the bracket on your curtain rod is not a thing of beauty, hide it with the flourish of a contrasting fabric tied like a handkerchief.*

ABOVE LEFT *If you choose a dramatic finial such as this snakelike example, both the pole and the drapery should be simple in contrast.*

LEFT *This rich, textured velvet drapery recalls a medieval hanging and has therefore been hung in appropriately historical fashion, using wide tabs to attach it to a narrow rod.*

BELOW *In a room dominated by classical moldings, the curtains have been hung in similar context, using the simplest of rings and poles and a classical, spear-headed brass finial.*

Swags and Cascades

Many draperies and windows are enhanced by the addition of swags and cascades, but the depth and length of each element of the design should be carefully worked out. The design of both swags and cascades should be fairly simple. A small window, for example, needs no more than one swag and a balancing pair of cascades, whereas up to three swags may be used on larger windows. You should also bear in mind that the more swags on any one window, the more prominent the accompanying cascades should be.

ABOVE *The swags and cascades at each of these windows create an asymmetrical effect.*

TOP LEFT *This traditional window is perfected by a swag and cascades in a gauzelike material, attached within the window frame.*

TOP CENTER, ABOVE RIGHT *A single drapery panel is attached to an iron pole and secured at the side of the window. A striped swag is caught over the pole and falls into an informal cascade.*

RIGHT *These are swags and cascades in the grand manner, with full-length draperies embellished by three swags and cascades. Rosettes hold each swag; the fringe accentuates the design.*

Swags and cascades can very often look effective above a pair of draperies in a different fabric. Rigidly classic swags, perhaps in a heavy silk, look good above sheer draperies at a tall window, while swags and cascades made from pieces of antique material are shown to advantage above plain draperies. If a window lacks any architectural interest, a well-designed arrangement of swags can make it look more inspiring. But whatever design you choose, from traditional swags and cascades to a piece of fabric draped informally over a pole, do not skimp on fabric. Properly made swags involve more material than you might think.

LEFT *This is a witty version of a traditional swag. The deep swag, which is caught in the center and edged with bobbles, hangs over two narrow strips of folded fabric and frames the view beyond.*

BELOW LEFT *The use of a luxurious yellow fabric is justified for such a formal arrangement.*

BELOW, BOTTOM LEFT *Used over sheer curtains, the sharply tailored swags and cascades of a formal dress curtain can make a feature of an otherwise architecturally unremarkable landing window. The geometric design of the fabric is echoed in the still life of branches arranged in terracotta urns on each side of the window.*

Valances and Cornices

One of the glories of 18th-century windows in grand houses were the wooden or plaster cornices, which were ornately carved and gilded. Like the crown of a picture frame, they straddled the window confidently, while from beneath them hung equally confident draperies or balloon shades. At the other end of the scale from these rather grand cornices were shades and simple draperies hung from behind a flat board made from wood that was either left unadorned or decorated with exquisite images of flowers and fruit on a painted background.

Although window treatments today are generally lighter in appearance, there are many situations in which draperies look far better with a valance or cornice, rather than just a heading. A valance or cornice is a defining and anchoring device and can give added importance to a window. However, the look of many windows is ruined by a top treatment that is out of proportion with the draperies below. Small windows with short curtains or draperies, for example, require no more than an apronfrill, while tall windows need a deep and relatively imposing valance of some distinction. A rough guide is that the valance should measure about one-sixth of the finished drapery length. Although this is a generalization, it provides a useful starting point for ideas. Valances can even be used on their own without a pair of draperies below or perhaps just with a plain shade to give definition to windows that would be overwhelmed by draperies.

Today, a gilded and carved cornice would cost a great deal to have made, although there

ABOVE *Here, an ornate valance follows the lines of a bay window. The shape of the window is further accentuated by the diamond-shaped panels that run along the edge of the valance.*

ABOVE LEFT *This stiffened valance is composed of curved panels, each of which repeats and draws attention to the motif on the draperies.*

RIGHT *Light, gauzelike draperies are held back with ropes that are attached to brackets on the architrave. The draperies are topped with a loose decorative swag in a richly colored fabric that is draped neatly over a heavy gilded pole. The color of the swag is identical to that of the rope, for a unified effect.*

FAR RIGHT *Rather unremarkable full, unlined draperies are brought to life with a stiffened valance that dips down in a sweeping curve.*

are still certainly many craftsmen skilled enough to make them. An easier option is to use a decorated wooden or resin cornice, which is cut to fit the width of the window, and shaped to suit the draperies. The panels can then be painted and decorated with appropriate motifs. You should be able to find a specialist designer who makes different styles of cornice, many of which are copied from original designs. It is not, of course, difficult to make cornices at home. The board could be cut into different shapes, whether scallops, squares, fans, or triangular points, either by penciling the shape you want directly onto the board and then cutting out the design with an electric saw or by making a paper template first. You could then decorate the board in any number of ways. For example, it might be painted, stenciled, papered, or even decorated with colored tapes, ribbons, or motifs from a child's scrapbook.

A wooden cornice—whether straight or shaped—can also be covered with the fabric used for the draperies. However, if you use a

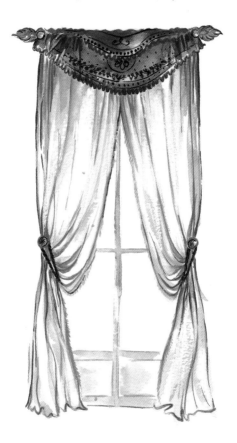

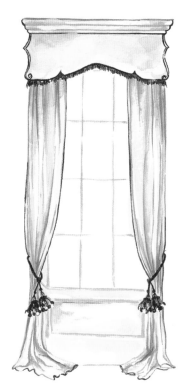

ABOVE *This softly draped valance is unusually deep, acting to correct the proportions and scale of a long, rather narrow window.*

TOP *Delicate unlined curtains fall from a molded cornice and deeply shaped valance.*

RIGHT *Gilded and carved cornice boards should be paired with relatively simple, subdued curtains.*

contrasting fabric, the rule is to balance a geometric with a floral, or a solid, design in colors that complement each other. Another treatment is to use the drapery fabric for the cornice but in a different way. For example, the central motif might be cut out and appliquéd onto a solid-colored background; or, with a geometric design of stripes, zigzags, or diamonds, the fabric could be cut out so that the pattern lies horizontally.

In contrast to a cornice, a valance is made entirely of fabric, although it is often hung from a piece of wood, called a valance shelf. In earlier times a shaped—or flat—valance was hung from beneath a wooden cornice, which might have been carved and even gilded. Such complicated arrangements are rare in modern window treatments, but a shaped valance can be very grand in itself. The valance is usually stiffened, with interfacing or interlining, and finished with a lining. As on a cornice, the lower edge may be shaped in whatever style seems appropriate to the treatment. It may also be trimmed with braid, piping, or fringe.

A softer, more informal option than a cornice or shaped valance is a pleated valance. This is normally hung from a curtain rod placed in front of the draperies—although it

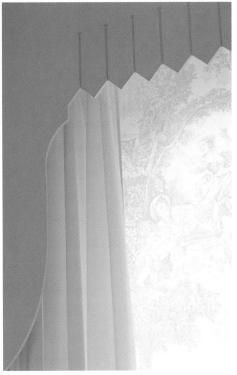

ABOVE *This valance is cut into different lengths, so that the vertical stripes act somewhat like a fringe while the draperies are edged with stripes.*

LEFT, TOP *A wooden cornice board hangs over a pair of draperies. The effect is subtle, rather than overdone, because the cornice board is the same color as the drapery fabric.*

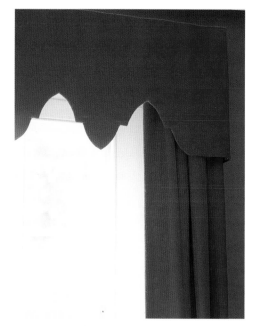

may instead hang from a valance shelf—and is pleated in the same style as used for them. If used with lined draperies, the valance should also be lined. In addition to such classic top treatments, many other effects are seen today. A piece of fabric may be casually draped over a rod, for example. Often this approach is used to show off an antique or handmade textile, which provides a striking contrast to the draperies. An old silk or paisley shawl can be draped into a swag to suggest antique richness.

ABOVE LEFT *This intricately shaped, fabric-covered cornice board is a modern version of a style popular in the 18th and early 19th centuries.*

ABOVE RIGHT *A cornice board made in the same fabric as the draperies is attached to the ceiling, hiding unattractive curtain rods.*

ABOVE *A narrow, stiff band against the ceiling is combined with a softer, pleated valance across the window and given added definition with a narrow trim above and below.*

ABOVE *Unusually—but possibly because the bed is a particularly fine example of the genre—this classical wooden four-poster has been left without hangings. To offset the relatively austere design, both the walls and the windows are hung with the same material. The valance is balanced by a deep border in a contrasting fabric.*

LEFT *A striking and exuberant chintz such as this must be treated with care when made into curtains because it is important that the all the elements be in proportion and to scale. Here, the full, very long draperies are balanced by a deep valance, which, crucially, has the dominant floral design carefully placed as a broad central stripe.*

Tiebacks and Brackets

By the 18th century, draperies were usually either caught back with an ornate confection of braids and tassels or restrained with fittings such as brackets, which had a more architectural quality. Both brackets and tiebacks are used extensively in window treatments today, and this is understandable.

You will find that antique brackets are rather expensive but, on the other hand, do hold their value. For a comparatively small outlay, they not only serve a practical and decorative purpose but can instantly alter the look of the draperies. A ready-made, overlong

drapery, for example, can be instantly adjusted, while a misshapen one may be greatly improved. Indeed, by scooping back the drapery fabric at any given point along its length, tiebacks and brackets create fullness and give the drapery additional shape.

In practical terms, they also allow as much light as possible into the room. In decorative terms, there is no limit to the uses for tiebacks and brackets, serving as they do to alter and pull together the look of both the curtains and the whole room. However, more importantly than for any other type of drapery accessory, you can correct the proportions of the drapery by carefully positioning a tieback or bracket.

Tiebacks and brackets can be either spartanly simple or dauntingly elaborate. The first design rule when deciding what to marry with a pair of draperies is to choose opposites: pair elaborate trimmings with simple draperies and vice versa. All too often draperies that are already overdesigned are burdened down with the weight of gilded tassels, braids, and other tiebacks, scooping the folds of fabric into heavy curves and loops. By all means add an eye-catching tieback such as an oversized tassel or a heavily gilded rosette, but use it with a simply designed drapery, perhaps in a

ABOVE A fabric tieback made in one of the same colors as the drapery has been padded to give it more impact.

TOP When a traditional rope-and-tassel tieback is used, it is important that it is heavy and thick enough for the weight of the drapery.

TOP LEFT A charming tieback idea is to use a contrasting piece of old or particularly pretty fabric simply tied like a scarf around the drapery.

LEFT A fabric tieback should be in proportion to the style of drapery it is designed to restrain.

material that is solid colored or has a self-striped pattern. Although using a heavy tieback with a drapery in a correspondingly heavy material can be successful, there is also an argument for using a weighty tieback with a fragile fabric, such as unlined silk, to create a dramatic contrast in both texture and weight. Single drapery panels can also benefit from the judicious use of a tieback, particularly when there is a sheer curtain or shade underneath.

Tiebacks were formerly often made from the same material as the draperies, although this approach now seems somewhat dated. They were either left unstiffened or shaped around a template, often in a curved or

scalloped shape. Another popular idea was to complete the tieback with a rosette of fabric, either in the drapery material or perhaps in a contrasting fabric. Rosettes were, in fact, used extensively in 18th- and 19th-century drapery design and can be very effective, although

ABOVE, RIGHT *The traditional tieback for a curtain is a cord and tassel—there is a huge variety available today in all price ranges. As with any sort of curtain tie, it is important that both cord and tassel be in proportion to the drapery, as well as being strong enough to hold the drapery firmly in place.*

they must be sufficiently generous and look more like a full-blown rose than a never-to-open bud. The tradition of *passementerie* has also given us cord or rope tiebacks that are often decorated with tassels. Plain or tasseled, they will look equally good on the right draperies. Like all tiebacks, they can either be secured to a hook fastened to the architrave or simply tied round the drapery itself.

Of course, there is no reason why you should have a traditional tieback or bracket in any case. With a lightweight drapery, a wide ribbon simply tied in a bow can look very striking, as can a hank of raffia on a pair of

draperies at French windows that lead into the garden. A natural-looking fabric can even be tied back using some thick, rough twine or unbleached rope. Also, if you are bordering a solid-colored drapery with braid, cord, or fringe, a simple tieback made from the same material as the border would create a strongly unified effect at the window.

In the past, brackets were very popular drapery accessories. They were either curved and cast in a metal such as brass—gilded ormolu for expensive draperies—or sometimes even carved in wood. Nowadays, brackets are usually made in either metal or wood, and

ABOVE *Skinny curtains such as these, hung at tall balcony windows, need skinny tiebacks to match. The thin metal brackets fit the bill perfectly.*

ABOVE LEFT *A flat band of material is discreetly but effectively embellished with a rosette made from the same material.*

LEFT *Braided cord makes one of the simplest of tiebacks and works best when used with a drapery made of fabric with a different texture.*

FAR LEFT *In some circumstances, this cord and tassel might be considered overelaborate, but paired with the glamorous silk-taffeta draperies, they are exactly what is required.*

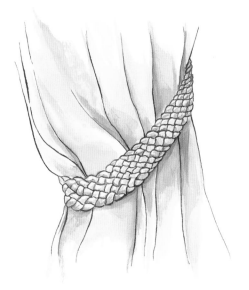

ABOVE *The coils of this rope blend with the stripes of the drapery in a particularly soothing way.*

ABOVE LEFT *A thickly textured tieback holds this heavy plain drapery in place.*

LEFT *Coiled textured cord used in a double loop hung loosely around a plain curtain gives an air of stylish informality.*

BELOW LEFT *A band of simply embroidered fabric makes a charming tieback.*

BELOW *A tieback in the same fabric as the drapery avoids detracting attention from the lines of the drapery itself.*

vary in design from the simplest, almost U-shaped, metal grip or loop to an ornately cast confection of classically inspired motifs from acanthus leaves to lions' heads. In addition to these traditionally shaped brackets that hold back the drapery in a firm embrace, there are also metal and wooden cloak-pin tiebacks. These consist of a short, straight peg ending in a disk, which is often cast in the shape of a rosette or other circular motif. The drapery then simply rests over the peg or is wound around it. Antique doorknobs in colored glass, brass, or wood can also look good, provided the shaft is long enough.

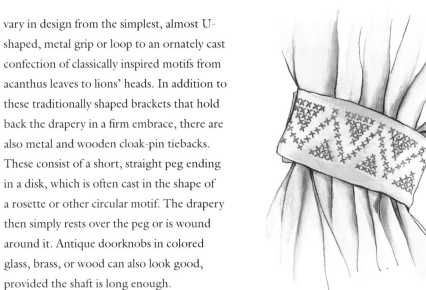

155

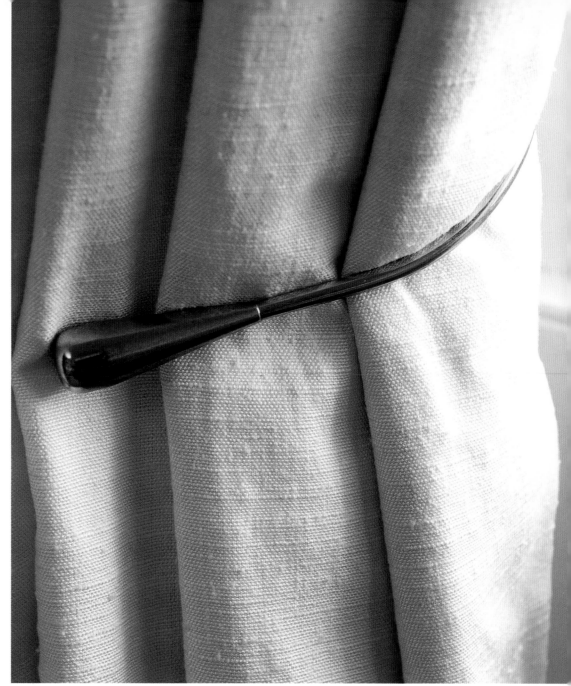

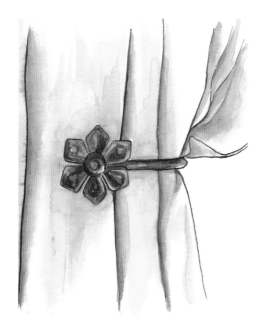

OPPOSITE (far left) *The iron pole is echoed by the curved iron tieback on these three-quarter-length curtains.*

OPPOSITE (top) *Easy to use and extremely effective, lengths of chain are wound neatly around the drapery in a traditional tieback fashion.*

OPPOSITE (center) *The positioning of any sort of tieback is crucial. Here a cord and tassel hang loosely in the center of the curtain, keeping the fabric in place without pulling it back.*

OPPOSITE (bottom) *The elegant curve of this horseshoe-shaped bracket, with its decorative finial, catches the light.*

ABOVE *A metal bracket that has the air of a comma, or a feather, lightly holds back this heavy white drapery in a subtle, restrained way.*

TOP LEFT *A three-dimensional tieback can be made with a bright ethnic necklace or, alternatively, with individual beads threaded into an appropriate design.*

ABOVE LEFT *Draperies made from a fabric that is as rich and luxurious as this look so much better when they are held back with a gilded peg rather than a tieback.*

LEFT *A decorative bracket allows for more precision in the draping of the material than a fabric or cord tieback.*

157

Decorative Trimmings

Well-made trimmings, or *passementerie*, such as braid, fringe, gimp, woven borders, bobbles, and ruffles, may seem expensive at first but are definitely worth the investment. Working braid or gimp into coherent designs in many colors or making a weighty tassel is a lengthy and complicated business. As usual, a sense of proportion is very important. A charming little bobble or piece of braid seen in a pattern book should be envisaged on a whole valance or swag or running around the edge of a drapery. Will it be dwarfed, or, conversely, will it overwhelm the drapery?

There is a wide choice of trimmings available, usually made from cotton, silk, or wool and combine varying colors and woven effects. Faced with such a selection, it is all too easy to regard trimmings as an instant salvation for a rather dull pair of draperies, and be tempted to choose everything. But this is an occasion when the maxim "less is more" holds true. Pin a sample of your chosen trimming onto the drapery fabric to see whether the draperies and the trimming work effectively together. In short, trimmings should contrast with and complement the drapery, defining its lines.

TOP LEFT *It is the contrast between the relatively heavy decorative trimming and the gauzy fragility of the red-and-white printed sheer curtain that gives this window treatment its charm.*

ABOVE, TOP CENTER, TOP RIGHT *Although fringe can be made to any length, it is important to match the length to the design of the drapery.*

ABOVE RIGHT *Fine pieces of embroidered textile such as this can be enhanced by the right choice of trimming.*

RIGHT *Two rows of crimson braid as well as a tasseled fringe are not too strong for intrinsically plain draperies.*

FAR LEFT (top) *This sophisticated border has the same striped theme as the material of the drapery and valance, only in miniature.*

LEFT *This border is highly successful because it complements, rather than contrasts with, the softly hued draperies.*

FAR LEFT (bottom), BOTTOM LEFT *This drapery is embellished solely with a band of braid.*

BELOW LEFT *On a Roman shade, a bobble fringe, dyed in the same color as the stripe, adds interest when the shade is raised.*

BELOW *Here, the fabric is cut to make a border shaped into a loose decorative scallop.*

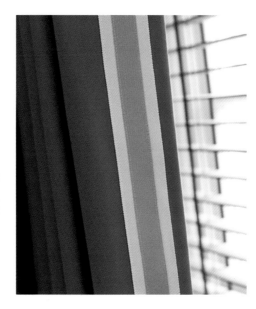

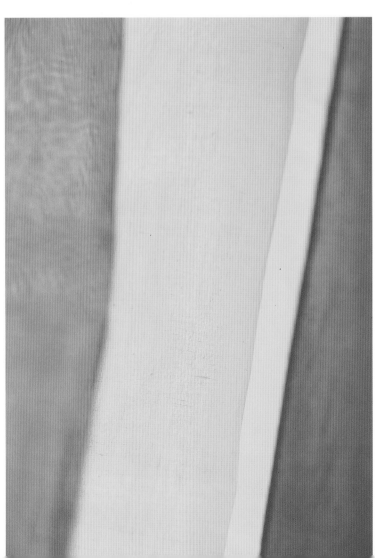

Practicalities

PRACTICALITIES

You may find that you need to make your own draperies, curtains, or shades because you have just moved into a new home; or you may simply enjoy designing your own window treatments. Whatever the reason, one of the most important considerations before embarking on any sewing project is to plan thoroughly what you intend to do in order to achieve the best results. For example, you should consider where you are going to work and what worktable or other surface you can work on, as well as decide on the best type of fabric to use and whether you will also need lining fabric. With careful measuring and cutting out, your home decorating projects should all run smoothly and successfully. This section outlines the basics of drapery and curtain making; clear instructions on stitches, seams, and other sewing methods are given in "Sewing Techniques," on pages 179–181.

MEASURING

This is the most important stage when making window treatments and should be considered carefully. The fabric quantity depends on the style of drapery or curtain, so you will have to decide whether you want them to be full length, over-sill length, or sill length (as the vertical arrows below indicate) and take accurate measurements. Curtains often hang inside the window recess, draperies generally outside it (as the horizontal arrows show). Other factors to consider include the heading style, the fullness of fabric, and any pattern repeat.

Heading Styles

When choosing a style of heading, you will have to consider the size of window, the style of window treatment, and whether the draperies (if used) are to draw or be stationary panels. If you are making draperies, you also need to decide whether to make the pleats by hand or to use one of the pleat tapes available. The commonest kind of pleat tape has pockets into which four-pronged hooks are inserted, which pull the fabric into folds. You can also buy tape containing cords, which pull it and the fabric into different kinds of pleats. However, if you are using heavy fabric or have a special effect in mind, you will need to make the pleats by hand. In some cases, calculating the positioning of pleats will be easier if you opt for a hand-pleated heading.

CALCULATING FABRIC QUANTITY

Each Fabric Length

Measure the finished length of the draperies and add the appropriate allowances for the hem and your choice of heading. For example, you will need 6 inches (15 cm) for a double bottom hem and 3 inches (7.5 cm) for a simple heading. The allowances are given where appropriate in the following pages. Allow extra material for patterned fabric by adding one repeat to each length.

Number of Fabric Widths

For draperies with heading tape:

1 Measure the length of the rod or pole and divide in half for two panels.

2 Add 4 inches (10 cm) for the side hems on one panel. Add another 4 inches (10 cm) for the overlap in the middle.

3 Multiply this width by the amount of fullness appropriate for the heading style. For example, simple shirring tape requires one-and-a-half times the rod length; cartridge pleat tapes two-and-a-quarter times the length; and pinch pleats two-and-a-half times the length. However, the fullness needed will be indicated by the manufacturer.

4 Divide this total width by the fabric width. Most fabrics are 47 inches (120 cm), 48 inches (122 cm), 54 inches (137 cm), 55 inches (140 cm) or 59 inches (150 cm) wide. Round off the resulting figure to the nearest whole number to work out the number of fabric widths each panel will take.

For draperies with hand-pleated headings:

1 Measure the length of the rod or pole. Divide in half for two panels. Add 4 inches (10 cm) for the side hems on each panel and another 4 inches (10 cm) for the overlap in the middle.

2 Work out the number of pleats and spaces that will fit the draperies with about 6 inches (15 cm) for each pleat and a space of 4¾ inches (12 cm) between each pleat. Divide the width of the panel

(minus the side hems and center overlap) by 4¾ inches (12 cm). Round off to the nearest number. So, if you have eight gaps, make nine pleats.

3 Work out the fabric for the pleats by multiplying the number of pleats by 6 inches (15 cm).

4 Add this figure to the total panel width (including the side hems and center overlap) and add an additional 4¾ inches (12 cm) for the return on the outer edge of each panel. (This will vary, depending on the position of the rod.) Round off to the nearest whole number.

5 Divide the resulting figure by the width of the fabric. Round off to the nearest whole number to find out the number of fabric widths for each panel.

Final Fabric Estimate

Multiply the overall panel length by the number of fabric widths for both panels to give the final fabric amount. Allow another 1 inch (2.5 cm) for every yard (meter) of non-preshrunk fabric.

CUTTING OUT THE FABRIC

Cut out all fabrics on a flat, clean surface. If you are using fabrics with a high sheen or a pile, mark the top of each length so that the texture will run in the same direction. Cut straight across the fabric at right angles to the selvage to ensure that the finished draperies hang straight. Make one end straight by pulling a thread across the weave and cutting along it, or use a right-angle triangle to mark a line on the fabric with a pencil and a rule.

Measure the length of the first width down each selvage and mark with pins. Fold the fabric along the pin line and cut along the fold. If the fabric has a large pattern, work out the length so that the hemline will come below a complete motif. It is much better to let a partial motif occur at the top of the draperies where it will not be so obvious. Cut the number of widths required for each panel in the same way. Make sure that on a patterned fabric each length starts at the same point and place half widths at the outer edges of the panels.

MAKING UNLINED DRAPERIES

Although most draperies hang better when they are lined, sometimes unlined draperies are more suitable. They are one of the easiest types of drapery to make and can produce sophisticated results. When estimating the fabric for unlined draperies, allow for a 6-inch (15-cm) hem and 2½ inches (6 cm) for each side hem. The heading allowance and total width will depend on the kind of heading tape you are using. The instructions that follow assume a 2¾-inch (7-cm) heading allowance.

1 Join widths and any half widths with a flat seam, matching the pattern if necessary. Trim off the selvages to prevent them from puckering the seam. Press each of the seams open.

2 Turn in and press double 1-inch (2.5-cm) hems along each side edge. Pin and baste these edges to within 2¾ inches (7 cm) of the top edge and 6 inches (15 cm) of the bottom edge.

3 Turn up and press 6 inches (15 cm) along the bottom edge. Press in a miter at each corner and then turn in and press the raw edge to make a double 3-inch (7.5-cm) hem. Machine-stitch the side hems, or sew by hand with a loose slipstitch. Stitch the mitered corners followed by the bottom hem, using the same loose slipstitch or catchstitch. Weight the draperies by sewing weighted tape into the hem or lead weights in the corners.

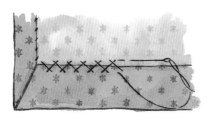

Adding Simple Shirring Tape

Loosely shirred headings can be used for very informal draperies made of lighweight fabric. You can buy strips of shirring tape, which measure 1 inch (2.5 cm) in depth and create a frill of fabric above the rod and loose gathers below. You can, of course, alter the depth of the upper frill by allowing for a deeper top hem.

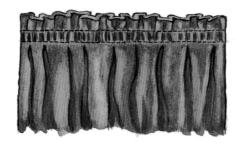

1 To apply the tape, turn down and press along the top edge of the fabric by 2¾ inches (7 cm), mitering the corners. Cut the tape to the width of the panel with another 2 inches (5 cm) for side hems. Turn under 1 inch (2.5 cm) of the tape at each end and pin and baste the tape to the wrong side so that the tape covers the raw edge of the hem.

2 Machine-stitch the tape along its top and bottom edges, stitching in the same direction. Sew the ends of the shirring tape in place by hand. Use the drawstrings to gather up the drapery so that it fits the rod; arrange the gathers evenly across the width of the drapery. Knot the strings at one end of the tape to hold the gathers in place. Fit hooks into the row of woven loops on the tape and hang the draperies from the rod.

Adding Cartridge Pleat Tape

Cartridge pleat tape, which gathers the fabric into thin vertical folds, is available in 3-inch (7.5-cm) and 4–5-inch (10–13-cm) widths, and in different weights for heavy and lightweight fabrics. This tape has three rows of pockets for inserting the hooks.

1 Cartridge pleat tapes are applied in much the same way as shirring tape, but the tape is positioned almost at the top of the drapery. If you wish, you can gather the tape first, before attaching it to the drapery, marking the position of the pleats on the tape with a pencil. Open out the tape and apply as usual. Do not put a pleat at the outer edges of the drapery, where a single hook will be.

2 Smooth out the tape and sew it to the drapery. Pull up the pleats again, according to your earlier pencil marks, secure the drawstrings, fit hooks into the loops, and hang the draperies from the rod.

MAKING LINED DRAPERIES

Lining draperies is important if you wish to protect the main fabric from sunlight and dampness and also to improve the hang of the drapery. Cotton sateen lining fabric is relatively inexpensive and is available in cream, beige, and white. In some places it is also possible to buy colored sateen to complement your drapery.

Standard Lining

This is the simplest method for lining draperies, but remember to add allowances on the drapery fabric for the side hems, the bottom hem, and your choice of heading tape. Cut out the lining to the size of the finished drapery and make sure that the drapery fabric is approximately 5 inches (13 cm) wider and 9 inches (23 cm) longer than the lining.

1 Join the widths and any half widths of drapery fabric and lining fabric as for standard unlined draperies. Place the lining on top of the drapery panel with right sides facing so that the top of the lining is 3 inches (7.5 cm) below the top of the drapery fabric. Pin the side edges of the drapery and the lining together as shown below and then machine-stitch ½ inch (1 cm) in from the edge. The stitching should run from 3 inches (7.5 cm) below the top of the lining to within 6 inches (15 cm) of the bottom edge. Remove the selvages or notch the seam allowances in order to reduce bulk.

2 Turn up and press 2 inches (5 cm) to the wrong side along the bottom edge of the lining. Make a double 1-inch (2.5-cm) hem and machine-stitch. Turn up and press 6 inches (15 cm) to the wrong side of the main fabric, press in the mitered corners, and baste a double 3-inch (7.5-cm) hem.

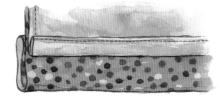

3 Turn the fabric and lining right side out, centering the lining to create an equal border of fabric along each side of the lining. Slipstitch the remaining side edges of the lining to the drapery, leaving some of the lining free at the top so that you can turn in the mitered corners of the main fabric.

Stitch the lower miters and hem of the drapery and remove the basting, as for an unlined drapery.

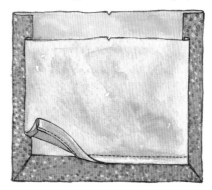

4 Turn down and press 3 inches (7.5 cm) along the top of the drapery, covering the lining, and press in and slipstitch the miters. Pin and baste the heading tape of your choice in place across the top of the drapery, following the instructions on page 164. Machine-stitch the heading tape in place.

Locked-In Lining
This particular lining method is preferred by professional drapery makers because it ensures that the draperies hang beautifully. When measuring for unfinished panels, make sure to allow an extra 5 inches (13 cm) in width and 9 inches (23 cm) in length than the finished flat drapery panel. The lining should be approximately 1¾ inches (4 cm) smaller all the way around than the drapery.

1 Join the drapery and lining widths as for draperies with an ordinary lining. Turn in and press 2½ inches (6 cm) down each side edge of the drapery and 6 inches (15 cm) along the bottom edge. Press in the miters at the bottom corners of the drapery. Loosely slipstitch the side hems, and sew the miters in place. Slipstitch or catchstitch the hem as for unlined draperies. Lay the fabric right side down. Draw a series of parallel vertical lines about every 12 inches (30 cm) using some tailor's chalk, or a pencil, and a yardstick.

Place the lining right side up on top of the drapery fabric so that its top edge is ¾ inch (2 cm) below the top edge of the drapery panel. Fold back one side edge of the lining lengthwise to the first chalk mark. Slipstitch or lock-stitch the lining to the

drapery, starting 7 inches (18 cm) down from the top of the drapery and joining them with large, loose stitches. Continue down the lining to the top of the drapery's bottom hem.

2 Smooth the lining out again. Fold back the other side edge of the lining to the next chalk line. Slipstitch or lock-stitch this line to the drapery. Repeat for each line across the drapery.

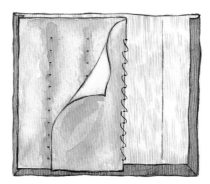

3 Turn in and press ¾ inch (2 cm) along the side edges of the lining and 1¾ inches (4 cm) along the bottom edge. Slipstitch the lining in place on the drapery along these three edges. Turn under and press 3 inches (7.5 cm) along the drapery's top edge and 2¾ inches (7 cm) along the top edge of the lining. Miter all corners, slipstitch in place, and then apply the heading tape of your choice.

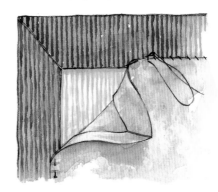

HAND-SEWN HEADINGS

Ready-made heading tapes achieve elegant results, but headings that are made by hand are neater, more precise, and more professional looking. There are a number of different styles to choose from, including pinch pleats, French pleats, and cartridge pleats, some of which are described here.

Pinch Pleats

These are by far the most popular kind of drapery pleat. You can buy tape to form these pleats, but making them by hand produces a crisper effect. The following instructions include an interlining. Though seldom seen in the United States, it produces a rich effect—and conserves heat. Table felt or flannelette can be used for this purpose.

1 To pleat the draperies by hand, measure the fabric quantities very carefully. You will need drapery fabric with a 4-inch (10-cm) bottom hem allowance and a 4-inch (10-cm) top hem allowance. Remember to include extra if you need to match the design on different widths of patterned fabric. When working out the number of fabric widths to buy, you will need to calculate the number of pleats and spaces that will fit each panel and also take the side returns, any center overlap, and the side hems into account (see "Calculating Fabric Quantity," page 163).

You will also need to make a lining panel measuring the width of the unpleated drapery with no side allowances, a ¾-inch (2-cm) top hem and a 1¾-inch (4-cm) hem allowance; a piece of interlining cut to the same size as the finished drapery panel, and a strip of interfacing cut to the same width as the finished drapery and at least 4 inches (10 cm) wide to ensure that the pleats maintain their shape.

2 Turn under 4 inches (10 cm) along the top edge of the drapery panel and position the top edge of the interfacing so that it lines up with the fold line. Catchstitch the interfacing to the drapery. Lay the piece of interlining over the interfacing, and lock-stitch in place. Turn the top edge and the

2-inch (5-cm) side hems of the drapery panel over the interlining, mitering the corners, and catchstitch. Turn up and stitch a ¾-inch (2-cm) double hem along the bottom of the lining and turn under and press ¾ inch (2 cm) along the top and side edges. Lock-stitch the lining to the interlining and slipstitch the folded top and side edges of the lining to the drapery panel.

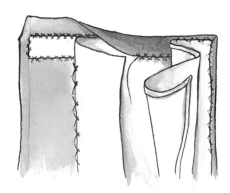

3 Turn up the 4-inch (10-cm) bottom drapery hem, mitering the corners as usual, and slipstitch the hem in place beneath the lining.

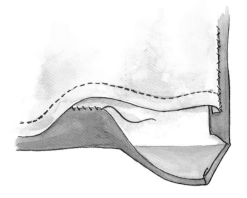

4 Using a pencil or tailor's chalk, mark the position of the returns, the pleats, the spaces, and the center overlap on the back of the panel according to your earlier calculations.

5 Fold and stitch the pleat lines to the depth of the interfacing. Form the pleats by hand and stitch to ½ inch (1 cm) below the interfacing. Stitch across the pleats at the top or hold in place with pin hooks.

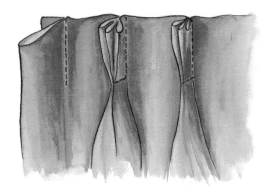

6 Fix hooks to the pleats and side edges. Hang from rings as shown or from traverse rod sliders.

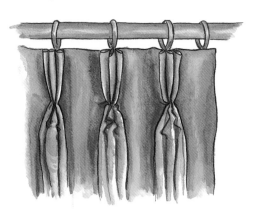

French, or Goblet, Pleats

Often used for stationary panels, French, or goblet, pleats can be decorated with cords, buttons, or tassels. Follow the instructions for pinch pleats, but once you have folded and stitched along the pleat lines, open out the pleats and hand-stitch around the base. Roll up strips of interfacing and wedge into each pleat to give it shape.

Cartridge Pleats

This simple-looking heading requires less fabric for each pleat but is made in the same way as pinch or French pleats. Follow the instructions for pinch pleats, again working out the number of pleats and spaces for each panel carefully, but after stitching the pleats, open them out fully and insert equal-size pieces of rolled-up interfacing into each to produce the neatly rounded shape.

Rod Casing

This type of heading is used for curtains such as tieback or fiberglass curtains. The casing simply runs across the top of the curtain and slips over a simple or adjustable curtain rod.

1 Measure the curtain material as for unlined draperies (page 164) and allow for a top hem of 4 inches (10 cm) and a bottom hem of 6 inches (15 cm). Unless you are using very sheer fabric, the width of the curtains should be about two times the length of the rod. If you are using extra-sheer fabric, allow more.

Join the widths of curtain fabric as for unlined draperies, making the side hems and double bottom hem as usual. Turn under and press 4 inches (10 cm) along the top of the curtain and make a double hem measuring 2 inches (5 cm) on the bottom. Machine-stitch along the bottom edge and then stitch a second line 1 inch (2.5 cm) above the first line. If you are using a thick rod, you will need to allow extra fabric to make a casing that is wide enough to take the rod and to ensure that the ruffle is in proportion to the rest of the curtain. As a rule, this measures about 1 inch (2.5 cm), so you should allow 2 inches (5 cm) for the double thickness.

2 Slip the rod or wire through the casing and hang the curtain.

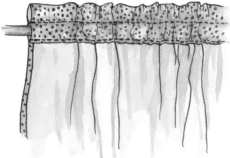

Scalloped Heading

This heading is fairly plain. The instructions are for a flat curtain; allow for fullness, if required.

1 Measure and make up the curtain as for unlined draperies (page 164) but leave the top and bottom edges unfinished. Allow only ¼ inch (5 mm) at the top of the panel for the hem. Work out how many scallops will fit across the panel, with each scallop measuring about 3 inches (7.5 cm). Allow for ¾ inch (2 cm) between each scallop and an equal amount of fabric on either side of the panel.

2 Make a scallop template by drawing a circle with a 1¾-inch (4-cm) radius on cardboard. Draw a

rectangle using the diameter of the circle as a base. The sides of the rectangle should measure 2½ inches (6 cm). Cut out the whole template.

3 Draw around the template along the width of the panel, on the wrong side of the fabric, with a pencil, leaving 1 inch (2.5 cm) between each scallop and equal spaces at either end.

4 Make a facing by cutting out a 6-inch- (15-cm-) wide strip of fabric, ½ inch (1 cm) longer than the width of the finished panel. Turn in each short end of the facing by approximately ¼ inch (5 mm). Press flat and baste along these ends. With right sides together, baste the facing to the top of the curtain. Turn up the bottom edge of the facing by ¼ inch (5 mm) and press and baste. With the wrong side of the curtain fabric facing you, baste through the panel and facing along the outline of the scallops, with a straight line of basting between them, about ¼ inch (5 mm) in from the edge. Machine-stitch along this basting line. Cut out the scallops, making sure to stop ¼ inch (5 mm) short of the stitching, and cut notches in the material to reduce bulk (see "Curved Seams," page 180).

5 Turn the curtain and facing right side out and press flat. Slipstitch the side and bottom edges of the facing in place. The curtain can be hung in a number of informal ways. You can simply sew metal curtain rings to the center of the spaces between each scallop as shown below. Alternatively, you can buy decorative metal clips that you fix onto both the curtain and the metal curtain rings. Slip the pole through these curtain rings. Hold the finished curtain up against the window in order to check the length of the hem, then pin, baste, and slipstitch the hem in place. Press the finished curtain, then slip the rings over your choice of pole. Hang the curtain.

OTHER DRAPERY STYLES

The following ideas show the wide variety of curtains and draperies that can be made.

Tab Headings

This is a simple heading style for a pair of curtains and is also suitable for wall hangings.

1 Make the curtains as usual, but leave the top and bottom edges unfinished, allowing only ½ inch (1 cm) at the top for a hem.

2 First find the length of the tab by measuring the circumference of the rod, adding another 3 inches (7.5 cm) for seam allowances. Each finished tab should measure about 2–3 inches (5–7.5 cm) in width with 1 inch (2.5 cm) for seams. Decide on the number of tabs you will need, as for scalloped headings. Make enough tabs so they can be spaced every 4 inches (10 cm) along the width of the curtain, starting 1 inch (2.5 cm) in from either end.

3 Cut strips for the tabs to the required length and width. Keeping right sides together, fold each strip in half lengthwise and make a ½-inch (1-cm) seam down the long edge, leaving the ends open. Turn right side out and refold so that the seam is at the back of the strip in the center. Press flat.

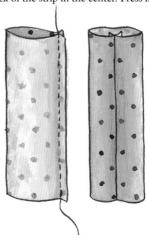

4 Fold the tabs in half widthwise and pin at the correct spacing to the right side of the curtain, matching the raw edges. Baste in place ½ inch (1 cm) from the edge.

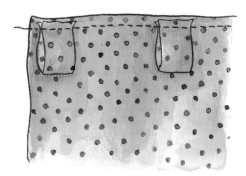

5 Cut a 3-inch (7.5-cm) strip of fabric ½ inch (1 cm) wider than the curtain to make a facing. Turn in ¼ inch (5 mm) on each short end, press, and baste. With right sides facing, baste the facing to the top of the curtain. Turn up ¼ inch (5 mm) along the bottom edge of the facing; press and baste. Baste and stitch along the top of the curtain ½ inch (1 cm) from the edge through all the fabric including tabs. Turn right side out and press flat.

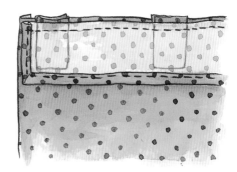

6 Slipstitch the side and bottom edges of the facing to the main fabric and slip the rod through the tabs. Temporarily hang the curtain to check the hem length. Pin and baste the bottom hem and slipstitch in place. Press flat before hanging.

Tab Heading with Buttons

You can create a variety of decorative effects with tabs. For example, the tabs can be made from material contrasting with the curtain or tabs in different colors can be alternated across the width of the curtain. You might also like to embellish the tabs with buttons, brocade, ribbons, or bows. These decorative effects are all easily achieved, particularly if you enjoy experimenting with different trimmings and finishes. The striking method shown below is ideal for full-length but informal draperies.

1 Make a curtain or drapery panel as usual and sew the tabs to the back at regular intervals.

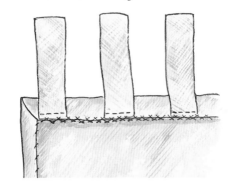

2 Fold the tabs to the front and sew a button to the center of each tab through all thicknesses.

3 Hang the curtain from a decorative pole.

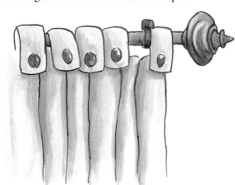

A Valance-Trimmed Drapery

Follow the instructions on pages 163 for measuring and cutting out the draperies. For the valance, cut out an extra length of both the drapery fabric and the lining to the same width as the drapery. The depth of the valance will depend on the length of the drapery, but allow approximately 10 inches (25 cm) for a 6-foot (2-m) drapery.

1 Make the draperies, leaving the top edges of the drapery fabric and the lining unfinished. With right sides together, sew the side seams of the valance and its lining. Turn right side out; press.

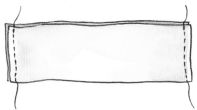

2 Placing the right side of the valance to the wrong side of the drapery, pin, baste, and stitch across the top of the drapery and valance, leaving a ½-inch (1-cm) seam allowance. Fold in each end of this seam and hand-sew to finish.

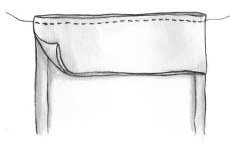

3 Turn the valance over to the right side of the drapery and press the seam. Finish the bottom of the valance by tucking the raw edges to the inside and sewing a length of fringe across it as shown.

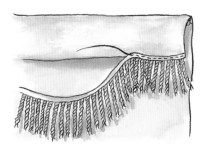

4 Sew approximately twelve rings to the top of the curtain and thread onto a wooden or cast-iron pole.

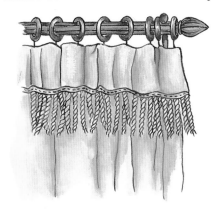

Other Valance Trimmings

You may like to sew a strip of bobbles across the bottom edge of the valance, or make both the drapery and the valance from sheer fabric (see below).

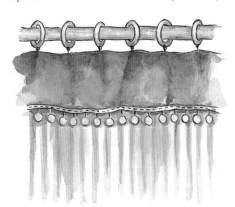

A Fixed Hook Portière

Follow the instructions on page 163 for measuring and cutting out draperies, leaving a ½ inch (1-cm) seam allowance. Allow approximately two times the width of the doorway for the drapery width. Line the portière with the same fabric or contrasting fabric to make it attractive from both sides.

1 With right sides facing, pin, baste, and stitch the two pieces of fabric together around the bottom and side edges with a ½-inch (1-cm) seam. Turn right side out and press flat. Make the loops by folding fabric strips in half lengthwise. Baste and machine-stitch in place between the fabric pieces.

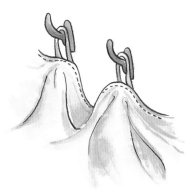

2 Hang the loops over hooks fixed to the door frame; hold the portière in place with a tieback.

Eyelet Headings

Eyelet headings are perfect for decorative curtains or draperies that are not pulled back very often. They are one of those simple but effective finishing touches that can turn the most ordinary window treatment into something special.

The eyelets can be threaded over a wooden or brass pole for an understated effect; or you can use string or ribbons threaded through the eyelets to suspend the curtains or draperies.

The headings should always be stiffened with a strip of interfacing for added crispness. The stiffening fabric is hand- or machine-stitched between the fabric and the lining or inserted into a folded heading. If your draperies are unlined, they will need a facing in order to hide the stiffening. You can buy the grommets used to finish the eyelets in a variety of sizes from most department stores or notions stores. They are accompanied by a small gun for punching the grommets through the fabric.

Simple Eyelets

Having stiffened the top of the drapery with a strip of interfacing when making the draperies, punch ¾-inch (20-mm) grommets through the fabric according to the manufacturer's instructions and thread onto a suitable pole.

Eyelets with Cords or Ribbons

When measuring for the drapery fabric, add 4 inches (10 cm) to the total drapery length. Turn under 2½ inches (6 cm) on the top edge of the drapery. Open out and place a 2-inch (5-cm) strip of interfacing against the fold line. Cover over the interfacing with the drapery fabric and slipstitch

into place. Once you have completed the draperies, punch ⅜-inch (10-mm) grommets into the fabric and thread double cords through them as shown.

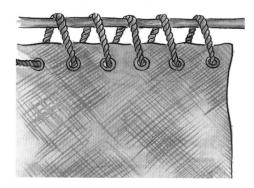

Alternatively, insert ¾-inch (20-mm) grommets and tie the drapery to the pole using 12-inch (30-cm) ribbons tied into bows as shown below.

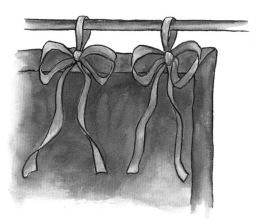

Shower Curtains

These are easy to make from waterproof fabrics; or use normal fabric with a plastic inner curtain. Most shower curtains should be made to a fullness of one-and-a-half times the length of the shower rod. A hemmed shower curtain can also have metal rings sewn along the top every 4 inches (10 cm), which can then be slid over a shower rod.

1 When cutting out the fabric and inner curtain, allow for 1-inch (2.5-cm) double side hems and a 2-inch (5-cm) double hem along the bottom. Add a ½ inch (1-cm) seam allowance across the top edge.

2 Turn under 1-inch (2.5-cm) double hems down the sides and a 2-inch (5-cm) double hem across the bottom edge of the fabric and inner curtain, mitering the corners, and stitch. Place the lining on

top of the fabric with right sides together and stitch a seam ½ inch (1 cm) below the top raw edges. Turn the fabric right side out and press the seams flat.

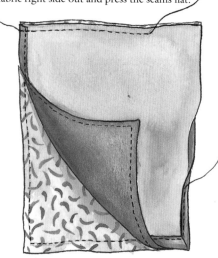

3 If the shower rod is not stationary, stitch a casing to accommodate it, positioning the upper row of stitching ½ inch (1 cm) from the top edge.

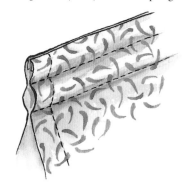

4 For an unlined shower curtain, turn under the top edge by 1 inch (2.5 cm) and insert grommets every 6 inches (15 cm) as shown below.

SWAGS AND CASCADES

Swags and cascades can be fixed to a shelf above the window although many are threaded on a second pole that extends beyond the curtain rod, or on the curtain rod itself. The method shown here uses a shelf fixed above the window as for valances (page 172). When making swags and cascades, use an old sheet to make a pattern. This will give a visual and mathematical idea of the degree of drape.

1 The upper edge of the swag piece should be about 10 inches (25 cm) shorter than the shelf, while the bottom edge should be about 8 inches (20 cm) longer, although this depends on the depth of swag you want. Pin the swag piece across the top of the shelf and gather the ends until you are happy with the effect. Mark the material with tailor's chalk where it folds over the front of the shelf, as well as the depth of the ungathered swag.

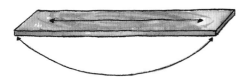

2 Open out the swag piece and mark the seam-lines, using the chalk marks as guides. Use this as a pattern to cut out the fabric, allowing for a 1-inch (2.5-cm) hem along the top and bottom edges and 1 inch (2.5 cm) for gathering and finishing down the angled sides. Make the swag and the lining as for normal lined draperies, treating the top and bottom edges of the swag as if they were the sides of a drapery panel.

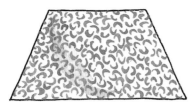

3 To make the pattern for the cascades, work out the width and spacing for the fold lines with a tape measure held against the shelf. Decide on the inner and outer lengths of the folds in the cascades. Transfer these measurements to the fabric pattern. Cut out the cascade pattern and check for fit.

4 Use the fabric cascade pattern in order to cut out the cascades from drapery fabric, allowing ¾ inch (2 cm) for seams around the sides and bottom edge and 4 inches (10 cm) along the top edge. Place the lining on top of the main cascade piece with right sides facing. Stitch all around the sides and bottom edges. Trim the seams, press, and turn right side out.

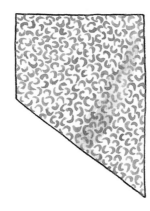

5 Run two rows of gathering stitches along the angled sides of the swag panel and pin to the shelf to check the effect. Staple to the top of the shelf.

6 Mark and press the pleats in place on the two cascade panels, using the fabric cascade patterns as a guide. Stitch the pleats by hand and staple the cascades to the top of the shelf as shown.

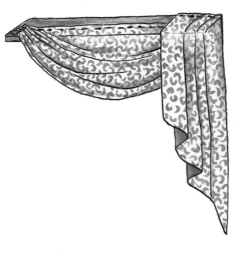

7 The swag and cascades can be used alone at a window or in conjunction with a pair of draperies. You can, of course, use different fabrics for the swag and the cascades to create dramatic effects.

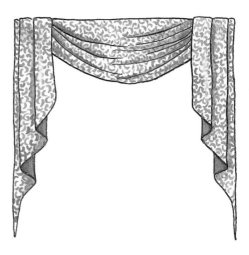

Swag Alternatives

There are a number of attractive ways of varying the classic swag and cascades just described. For example, a swag does not necessarily have to be accompanied by a pair of cascades. You may simply prefer to make the swag and cascades from one large piece of fabric, as shown below, draping the fabric over a pole and stapling it in place. The look can be harmonized still further by adding a decorative trimming, such as fringe, bobbles, or braid, along the edge of the swag and down the inside of the cascades. Alternatively, you could stitch the swag to a pair of straight draperies made with a rod casing.

VALANCES

Valances can be fixed to a shelf above the window frame and made in a variety of styles—straight, shaped, gathered, or pleated. You can design the shape of the valance after the shelf is up, making sure that the shelf is wide enough to cover the width of the window frame. A general rule of proportion is that the valance should be up to one-sixth of the height of the window, but for a more dramatic effect, you can make it a little deeper.

Cutting Out the Fabric

For a shaped valance, cut out the main fabric so that it is approximately 2 inches (5 cm) larger than the template all the way around (see "Making a Template"). Cut out a piece of lining, interlining (optional), and interfacing, all the same size as the template.

Fixing the Shelf

First decide on the position of the shelf. You can either fit it close to the frame around the window or make it wider and fit it above the window, in order to make the window seem larger. The draperies themselves will hang inside the box, so make sure that there is enough room for the draperies to stack back when opened.

Fit the shelf with angle irons, or screw it directly to the wooden window frame if possible. Use ½-inch (1-cm) plywood or softwood that is at least 4 inches (10 cm) wide. Cut the wood to the same length as the curtain rod, adding another 2 inches (5 cm) for clearance. To create the box, screw 4-inch- (10-cm-) square pieces of wood to each end of the shelf before fixing the shelf in place.

Making a Template

Make a pattern for the valance by trimming a sheet of paper a little larger than the finished length of the valance including the two side pieces. Fold in half down the center. Draw the shape along the bottom of the folded paper and cut out. Unfold the paper and try it against the board for size and effect.

If you are making a gathered or pleated valance with heading tape, remember you will have to elongate any shaping you design to allow for the fullness of the fabric. To do this, cut a second paper template to the finished size of the valance before gathering. Take measurements down the length of the first template, every 4 inches (10 cm) or so, and transfer these to the second one. Spread these measurements apart on the second template as appropriate for the heading tape. Some pinch pleat tapes, for instance, need two-and-a-quarter times the finished width, so allow for this when transferring the shape to the second template.

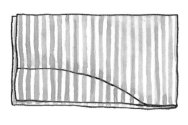

Making a Shaped Valance

1 Lock-stitch the piece of interlining (optional) to the wrong side of the main fabric. Center the interfacing over the interlining and catchstitch in place all around the edge.

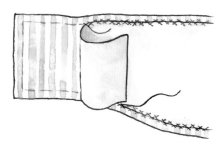

2 Fold the seam allowance of the main fabric over the interfacing, mitering the corners. Clip the seam allowance and catchstitch in place.

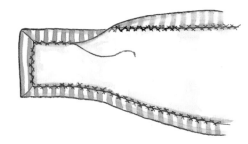

3 Turn under the seam allowance all around the lining so that it is about ½ inch (1 cm) smaller than the main panel of the valance. Slipstitch the folded hem of the lining to the seam allowance all the way around the main panel. Glue one strip of hook-and-loop tape to the edge of the shelf and stitch the other strip to the back of the valance for sticking directly to the board. Fix the valance to the shelf.

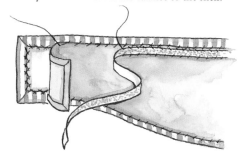

4 There are a variety of ways in which you can fix the valance to the board. For example, you can use ½-inch (1-cm) tacks, which are then concealed with a strip of fabric or braid. The fabric is simply glued over the tacks with a special fabric glue. You can also use screw eyes, which are fitted around the outer edge of the underside of the shelf, from which you hang hooks fixed to the inside of the valance.

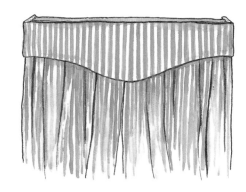

Decorative Alternatives

Valances are the ideal way to add a personal touch to a window treatment. Shaped valances enable you to devise your own imaginative designs, which are easy to apply to a template. Choose from among the ideas shown below, which range from curved valances to those with zigzag points. Valances can also be pleated or gathered to create a decorative effect across the top of a plain pair of draperies. Both shaped and pleated or gathered valances can be edged with trimmings.

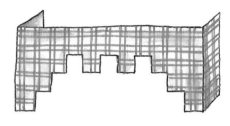

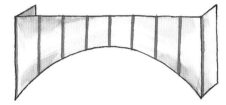

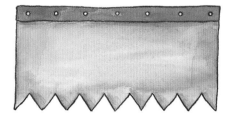

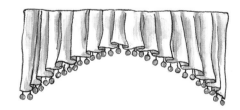

A Gathered Valance

For a gathered valance you will need a piece of fabric measuring twice the finished width of the valance plus a piece of fabric cut the same size as the finished width for the top border. You will also need a similar amount of lining, a piece of contrasting fabric to edge the bottom of the valance, and some interfacing to stiffen the top border.

1 Make the top border as you would a shaped valance (page 172) but leave the lower edge straight and unfinished.

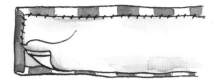

2 Add a band of contrasting fabric, which should measure approximately 3 inches (7.5 cm) in depth, to form a border along the bottom of the gathered part of the valance.

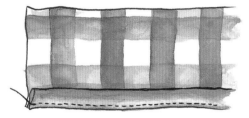

3 Sew a lining to the side edges of the gathered part of the valance as you would a conventional drapery with a standard lining (page 164) but leave the top edge and stitch the hem.

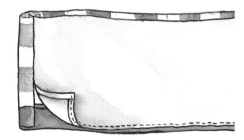

4 Sew two rows of gathering stitches about ½ inch (1 cm) down from the top edge of the gathered part of the valance. Draw the stitches up in order to create the gathers until the valance is the right width for the top border.

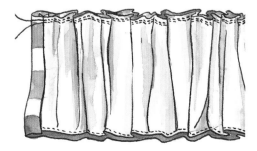

5 Pin, then machine-stitch together the top border and the gathered edge of the valance with right sides together. Stitch through both the main fabric and the lining of the gathered section but only through the main fabric of the top border.

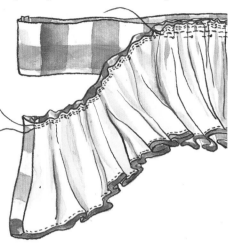

6 Tuck the seam allowances into the lining of the top border and hand-stitch to finish.

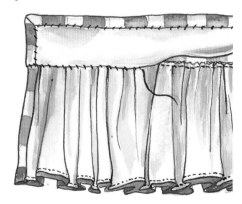

7 Press the valance, paying special attention to the gathered part. If you are using hook-and-loop tape, sew it 1 inch (2.5 cm) from the top of the valance. Attach the valance to the shelf.

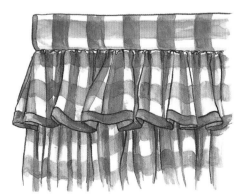

SHADES

Practical and decorative, window shades keep out the light and protect delicate fabrics.

Roller Shades

These are the simplest shades to make and consist of fabric wound around a wooden roller attached at the top of the window. The shade can be pulled down to produce a flat screen over the window. When released it winds around the roller unless locked into position. Roller shades are ideal for sloping windows and can be secured at the bottom with a hook. Roller-shade kits typically contain a wooden roller with a square pin at one end and a round pin attached to a pin cap; two brackets for fixing the roller in place, either to the side or the front of the window frame; a wooden batten for slipping through the casing; a cord holder and cord for adjusting the level of the shade.

To work out the amount of fabric, measure the length of the window and add 8 inches (20 cm) for the batten casing as well as enough fabric to cover the roller when the shade is down. To find the width of the roller and fabric that you need, measure the width of the window and add 2 inches (5 cm) to each side. If you want the shade to hang inside the recess, measure the width of the window and subtract the space needed for the brackets. You probably will not be able to buy a kit to fit the exact dimensions of the shade so buy the next size up.

Cutting Out the Fabric

There are special fabrics available for shades that do not fray and are stiff and fade resistant, although ordinary fabrics can be stiffened with a liquid or aerosol stiffening agent. If you decide on this method, test a piece of sample fabric to see how it responds and stiffen the fabric before cutting out in case of shrinkage. Cut out the fabric for the shade to the measurements of the roller, making sure that you cut the fabric out straight (a right-angle triangle is useful here), so that the shade will hang correctly and roll up freely. If you dislike the raw edges, turn in a narrow hem on each side edge before stiffening the fabric and bond with fusible web.

Assembling the Roller Shade

1 Fix the metal brackets to the wall or window frame, depending on how you have decided to hang the shade. Often, the square, slotted bracket is positioned on the left and the round-hole bracket on the right so that the rolled-up fabric is visible at the top, but check the manufacturer's instructions first.

2 Measure the distance between the brackets to find the length of the roller and the wooden batten, then cut them down to size. Position the metal end plate, which comes with the roller-shade kit, over the cut end of the roller and tap in the pin.

3 Cut out the fabric, then turn over and stitch a casing across the bottom of the shade, deep enough to take the wooden batten. Insert the batten into the casing.

4 Attach the cord and cord holder with screws to the wooden batten as shown below.

5 Turn over a narrow allowance at the top of the shade. With the right side of the fabric facing you and the round pin on the right, roll the turned edge over the roller and fix in place with ¼ inch (5-mm) tacks spaced approximately every 2 inches (5 cm). Roll up the shade and then hang it by attaching it to the brackets. To test the shade, pull it down and then remove it from the brackets. Roll it up halfway, hang, and pull it down again. Keep taking the shade down and rolling it up until it will roll easily to the top of the window when released.

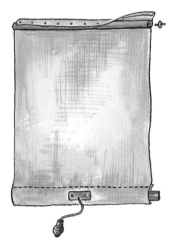

Decorative Edgings

Roller shades can be decorated with a variety of trimmings such as ribbons, fringe, or braid. Stiffened fabric is difficult to pin, so simply tape the ribbon or fringe to the wrong side of the shade, stitch through the tape and fabric, and then remove the tape. An equally attractive, but slightly more complicated, alternative is to shape the edge of the shade, as described below.

1 Sew a tuck about 3–6 inches (7.5–15 cm) from the edge of the shade for the wooden batten, thus leaving a strip of fabric below the batten.

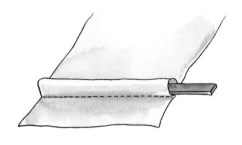

2   Take a piece of paper the same size as this edge. Fold in half, draw the design, and cut out.

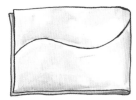

3   Open out the pattern and tape it to the wrong side of the edge. Pencil around the shape, cut out neatly, and finish with zigzag stitch.

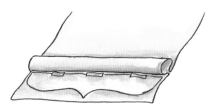

4   You can make other edgings using different template designs. Fold the paper accordion style, draw the design on the top, cut out, and trace.

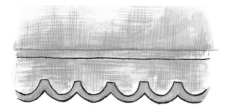

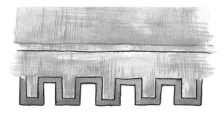

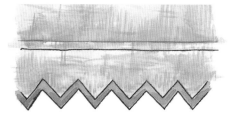

Roman Shades

Roman shades, which come in a number of styles, are operated by a system of vertical cords slotted through ringed tapes at the back of the shade. Roman shades can either hang outside the window frame, so that the entire frame is covered, or fit into the recess of the window. In the latter case, they can perhaps be combined with curtains.

To make a standard Roman shade, you will need two pieces of fabric measuring the width and length of the window, but add another 3½ inches (9 cm) to the length and 4½ inches (11.5 cm) to the width if the shade is to hang outside the window frame (if it is to hang inside the frame, add only 1 inch [2.5 cm]); shade tapes (there are a variety of tapes available with loops or rings fixed at regular intervals); nylon shade cord to thread through each vertical row of loops (each length should be twice the shade length plus one width); screw eyes (you will need as many as there are rows of tape); a wooden batten, measuring ¾ x 2 inches (2 x 5 cm) thick; a lath, measuring 1¼ inches (3 cm) wide; hook-and-loop tape; angle irons for fixing the batten to the wall or window frame; and a wall cleat.

1   The Roman shade is fitted to the batten, so cut the batten to fit the width of the window and hang it from angle irons fixed to either side of the window frame. Using a staple gun or tacks, secure the toothed side of a strip of hook-and-loop tape to the top of the batten.

2   Take the two pieces of fabric, and, with right sides facing, pin, baste, and machine-stitch them together along the two long edges and one of the short edges, leaving a seam of ½ inch (1 cm). Turn right side out and press flat. Cut two pieces of ringed or looped shade tape the same length as the shade. The first ring or loop should be placed 6 inches (15 cm) from the top of the shade. Pin these pieces of tape along each side of the shade near the edge. Machine-stitch in place. Space the remaining tapes at intervals of approximately 12 inches (30 cm) between the first two tapes. Check that the loops on all the tapes are level across the width of the shade. Cut the tapes to length, pin, and machine-stitch.

3   Turn under ½ inch (1 cm) along the bottom edge and then another 1½ inches (4 cm) to enclose the ends of the tapes. Press and machine-stitch, taking care not to catch the rings or loops while stitching. Machine-stitch the hem close to this folded edge. Insert the lath into the casing and secure the ends with hand stitching. Turn under ½ inch (1 cm) along the top of the shade. Pin, baste, and machine-stitch the other portion of the hook-and-loop tape to conceal the raw edge of the fabric.

4   Cut the nylon cords to length for each tape. Tie one length of cord to the bottom ring of each row of tape and thread the cord up through every ring to the top ring. Fix a screw eye to the bottom edge of the batten above each row of tape. Attach the shade to the top of the batten with the hook-and-loop tape and run the cords through the screw eyes to meet on the far left. Trim the cords to length and knot together. Fix the batten above the window with angle irons. Screw the cleat to the window frame so that the cords can be secured.

BED FURNISHINGS

If you have a four-poster bed, the draperies can hang down each post or close around the bed. You can also include a valance around the top of the bed. If you want to create the effect of a four-poster with an ordinary bed, you will have to improvise by hanging poles from the ceiling joists or by fixing a curtain rod directly to the ceiling.

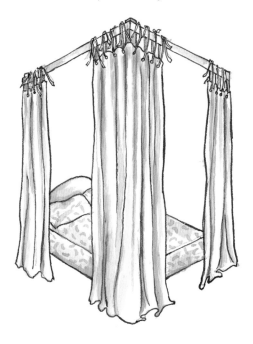

Dressing a Four-Poster Bed

1 First work out the amount of fabric for each drapery panel. To do this, measure the drop from the top of the post to floor level to determine the length and the distance around one corner of the bed to find the width. The distance will depend on how far you would like the draperies to draw around the bed. Use about one-and-a-half times the fabric fullness. Add a 4-inch (10-cm) top hem to the main length. You will also need a 2-inch (5-cm) strip of interfacing.

2 Make each drapery panel as for unlined draperies (page 164) but turn over the top edge by 2½ inches (6 cm). Open out and place the 2-inch (5-cm) strip of interfacing against the fold line. Cover the interfacing with the main fabric and slip-stitch in place. Punch ¾-inch (20-mm) grommets through the fabric and interfacing. Thread ties or ribbons through each eyelet and tie over the poles.

Corona Draperies

There are a variety of corona draperies to choose from which are fixed at the head of the bed. Corona draperies may be draped over a pole fixed either to the ceiling or to the wall; or they may be gathered and fixed to a coronet or semicircular bracket.

Simple Corona Draperies

1 The canopy is draped over a pole (fixed to a pole holder screwed to the ceiling joist or to a bracket in the wall) at right angles to the bed. The pole should be about 2 feet (60 cm) long, for which one width of fabric measuring 48 inches (122 cm) should be enough. If you would like more fullness, use more fabric widths and an equal amount of lining.

2 Measure from the top of the pole to the floor. Add at least 12 inches (30 cm) for looping the draperies into the tiebacks, plus 1 inch (2.5 cm) for the hem and ½ inch (1 cm) for the top seam. Double this measurement; multiply by the number of widths to find out how much fabric you need.

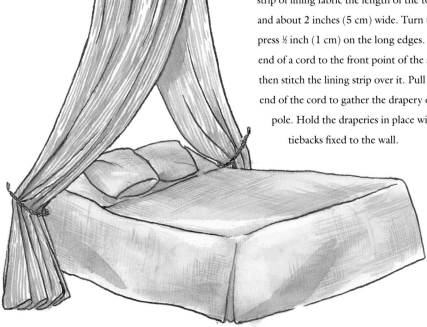

3 Cut the fabric into two equal lengths. If you would like extra fullness, cut two widths for each side and join the widths lengthwise, right sides facing, with a ½-inch (1-cm) seam; match the pattern if necessary. Remove the selvages, or cut notches in it, and press the seams flat. Lay the two pieces of material flat with right sides together and join across the top with a ½-inch (1-cm) seam. Make a panel of lining in the same way.

4 With right sides facing, stitch the lining to the main fabric along the sides edges, taking a ½-inch (1-cm) seam allowance. Turn right side out and press flat. Turn 1 inch (2.5 cm) to the inside along the bottom edges and slipstitch the edges of the lining and main fabric together. Cut a strip of lining fabric the length of the top seam and about 2 inches (5 cm) wide. Turn under and press ½ inch (1 cm) on the long edges. Sew one end of a cord to the front point of the seam, then stitch the lining strip over it. Pull the free end of the cord to gather the drapery over the pole. Hold the draperies in place with tiebacks fixed to the wall.

Coronet-Fixed Corona Draperies

These draperies, which are made up of a back drapery and two side draperies, hang from a coronet or semicircular bracket fixed to the wall usually 4–5 feet (1.2–1.4 m) above the bed. For a twin bed you will need two fabric widths for the back drapery; and for a double bed, three widths. Allow one or one-and-a-half widths for each side drapery, depending on how full you wish them to be.

1 Fix the coronet bracket to the wall with an angle iron. The bracket used here is made of 1-inch (2:5-cm) particleboard, measuring 16 inches (40 cm) across and about 10 inches (25 cm) deep. It has a curtain rod fixed to it so that the bed draperies can be made like ordinary draperies.

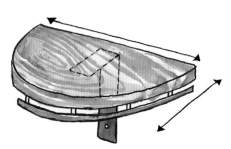

2 Measure the length of the draperies from the rod to the floor as for simple corona draperies. The draperies can either fall level with the floor or fall in staggered folds, as shown in the illustrations above. If you would like the draperies to fall in staggered folds, measure the edge of the side draperies against the wall as for corona draperies. If, on the other hand, you would like them to fall level with the floor, measure along the front edge of the side draperies instead. Add a 2-inch (5-cm) hem allowance and 1-inch (2.5-cm) top seam allowance to this initial length.

Draperies that fall in staggered folds

Draperies that are level with the floor

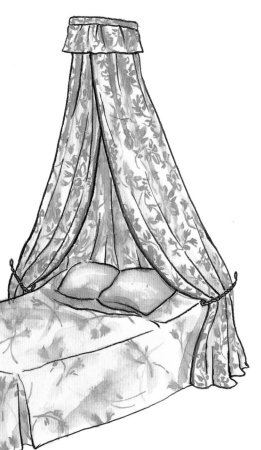

3 Make the back and side draperies as one large drapery, using the main fabric for both sides of the side draperies so that they look attractive from inside the bed. Use both the main fabric and the lining for the back drapery, with the lining facing the wall. Leave the hem unfinished if it is to hang level with the floor. Use shirring tape to gather the top edge. Gather the draperies to fit the coronet and hang the draperies from the rod. Screw ring holders to the wall for the tiebacks.

4 Mark the position of the tiebacks on the seamline between each side drapery and the back drapery. Unpick the seam here for about 6 inches (15 cm). Slipstitch the two layers of fabric around the slot.

5 Hang the draperies and attach the tiebacks. If the draperies are to hang level with the floor, mark the hemline with pins. Remove the draperies from the rod and cut 2 inches (5 cm) below this line. Turn up a double 1-inch (2.5-cm) hem.

6 Make a valance for the corona bracket, which consists of a flat panel about 3½ inches (9 cm) deep and a 4½-inch (11-cm) ruffle. Tack or staple the valance to the top of the bracket as shown.

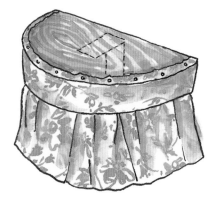

A Half Canopy

1 The total length of fabric should measure from the floor to the height at which the canopy will be attached to the wall (this will depend on the height of the ceiling but will be approximately 7 feet [2.2 m] from the floor) plus the length of the bed. Use a fabric that looks good from both sides, either plain or a woven pattern, and is the same width or wider than the bed, so that it will not be necessary to join fabric widths.

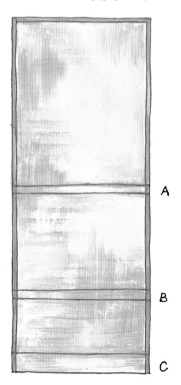

2 Cut the fabric to the width of the bed. Bind both long sides and the short side that goes down to the floor with bias binding (page 181).

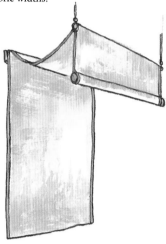

3 At point B make a casing in the fabric large enough to receive a ¾-inch- (2-cm-) diameter dowel. At point C (the unfinished end of the canopy), turn the hem up so that it is wide enough for another ¾-inch (2-cm) diameter dowel.

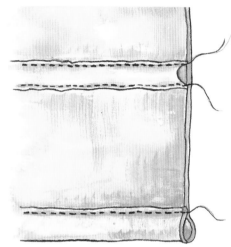

4 At point A sew the soft part of a strip of hook-and-loop tape, ½ inches (3.5 cm) in width, to the other side of the fabric across the width of the whole canopy. Screw a 1½ x ½ inch- (3.5 x 1 cm-) wooden batten to the wall at the correct height from which to hang the canopy. Staple the other part of the hook-and-loop tape to this wooden batten as shown below.

5 Feed the dowel through the casing at point B. It should protrude by 1 inch (2.5 cm) on either side of the canopy. Drill a small hole at each end of the dowel and attach two rings as shown. Thread the cords through the top rings. Attach the canopy to the wall with the hook-and-loop tape, and hold up the cords to calculate the exact position to screw two hooks into the ceiling to suspend the other end of the canopy. Feed the second dowel through the end casing in the hem. This should be cut to exactly the same width as the canopy.

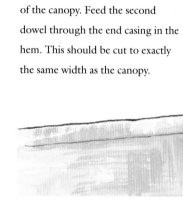

SEWING TECHNIQUES

The basic sewing methods shown here are not intended to be comprehensive, but they cover the most important techniques for making the curtains, draperies, and shades described in "Practicalities."

STITCHES

This range of stitches will enable you to achieve a professional finish when sewing any window treatment. Although much of the work is done by machine, there are places where hand stitching is essential. It allows for greater precision and hence better finished results. You can start and finish stitching with either a double backstitch or with a knot.

Running or Gathering Stitch

This hand-worked stitch is used mainly for gathering fabric or for basting. It is not a strong stitch, so it should not be used to sew seams. If a seam is too awkward to reach with a sewing machine, and you need to sew it by hand, you should use backstitches.

Secure the thread with a backstitch and sew small, regularly spaced stitches along the fabric. For basting, the stitches can be fairly large.

When using running stitches to gather a piece of fabric, such as for a gathered tieback, valance, or a simple decorative ruffle, sew two parallel lines of stitching approximately ¼ inch (5 mm) apart on either side of the seamline. Make sure that both threads are securely fastened at the starting point. Leave the finishing ends loose. Gather up the fabric as evenly as possible to the required length, sliding the fabric gently over the gathering threads. Secure the loose threads by twisting them in a figure eight around a pin and adjust the gathers if necessary.

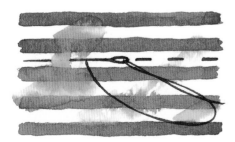

Backstitch

Working from right to left, insert the needle approximately ⅛ inch (3 mm) behind the spot where the thread came out. Bring the needle out again the same distance in front of this point. Continue by inserting the needle in the end of the last stitch.

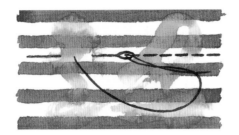

Catchstitch

This is a firm hemming stitch that is suitable for draperies and is used over any raw edge that will then be covered by another layer of fabric. Working from left to right of the material, secure the thread with a small stitch and bring the needle up through the fabric approximately ⅛ inch (3 mm) above the edge of the hem. Take the needle diagonally down to make a small backward stitch, from right to left, in the hem just below the edge. Bring the needle diagonally back to the fabric again and make another backward stitch in the fabric. Make sure that the thread is fairly loose while you work.

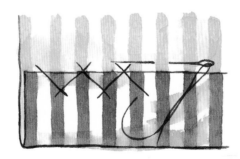

Lock Stitch

This is a particularly useful stitch, somewhat like catchstitch, although the thread is left very loose. It is used to hold linings and other fabric layers together where they must retain a degree of movement and flexibility.

1 After you have folded back and secured the lining or interlining to the main fabric with pins, fold back the lining to the first row of pins. Secure the thread at the top and make a stitch through the folded lining and the main fabric, picking up only a few threads with each stitch.

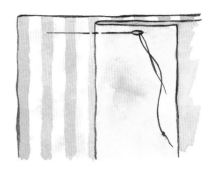

2 Make the next stitch about 2 inches (5 cm) farther along and bring the needle out over the thread to produce a loop. Keeping the thread very loose, continue down the length of the row.

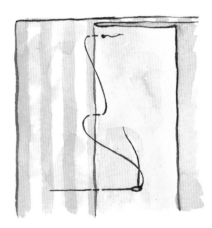

Slipstitch

This is often used to stitch the folded edge of a lining to the main fabric. Use a thread that matches the main fabric. Working from right to left, make a small stitch in the main fabric and insert the needle immediately into the fold as close as possible to the previous stitch. Pull the thread through. This should be done in one continuous movement.

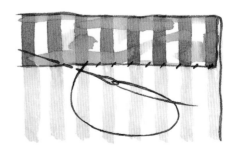

SEAMS

The look of your fabric furnishings will be marred by puckered or badly finished seams. Make sure that the raw edges are even before you start sewing, so that the seam allowances are the same.

Flat Seams

1 Pin, baste, and machine-stitch the right sides of the material together. Reverse the stitching at the ends of the seam to secure it. As a guide, you could insert horizontal pins ⅝–¾ inch (1.5–2 cm) from the raw edge and more pins at right angles, halfway between them. Machine-stitch, but remove the horizontal pins as the presser foot reaches them.

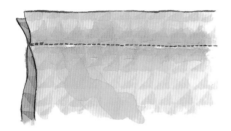

2 Remove all pins and basting, open out the seam, and then press open for a neat finish.

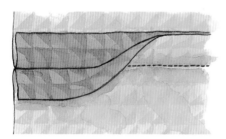

Curved Seams

Trimming curved seams serves to reduce bulk where the seams cannot be pressed open. Pin and stitch as usual but clip outward curves at intervals and cut V-shaped notches along an inward-curving seam. Press the seam open.

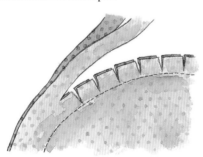

French Seams

This self-finishing seam encloses raw edges, but it can be bulky, so use it only on sheer or lightweight fabrics and only on straight edges.

1 With the wrong sides of the fabric together, sew a narrow seam. Trim off the seam allowance. Fold the fabric over the seam and press flat. Stitch again, about ½ inch (1 cm) from the first seam.

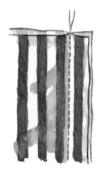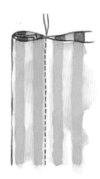

Lapped Seams

This seam is ideal if you wish to match the pattern on the right sides of two pieces of fabric.

1 Turn under one edge of the fabric by ½ inch (1 cm) and pin it in place over the other piece of fabric, matching the pattern where necessary.

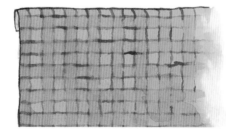

2 Pin and machine-stitch along the fold line on the right side of the fabric.

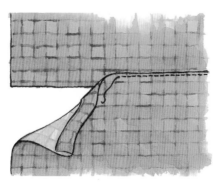

3 Sew another seam parallel to the first to catch down the raw edge underneath.

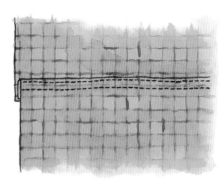

MITERING CORNERS

You will need to miter a corner when turning up a hem at a corner. In fact, mitering is the neatest way of working hem corners. This mitering method is also suitable for hems of unequal length, as is so often the case while making draperies where the bottom hem is deeper than the side hems. Borders and edgings also look much better when mitered.

1 Turn up the hems along the bottom and side edge of the fabric by the amount specified in the instructions. If you are basting the side hems first, do not pin and baste right up to the hem, so that you have enough fabric to fold over. Press and open out the folds. Fold in the corner diagonally so that the second fold lines match up. Press flat.

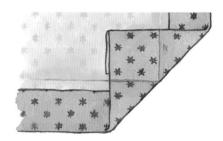

2 Trim down the corner between these matching points as shown below.

3 Fold the edges in place and slipstitch the seam, working inward toward each of the corners.

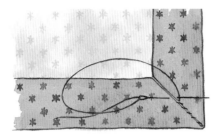

4 This method also works well for draperies that have side hems and a bottom hem of different depths. Simply slipstitch the corner hems where they do correspond.

BINDING

Binding is a simple yet effective method of finishing raw edges and also provides an attractive border for a drapery, shade, or other accessory. There are two types of binding: straight and bias. Both types are available ready-made, although in many cases you can achieve a more professional finish by making the binding yourself. On a curved or diagonal edge, bias binding must be used.

Applying Straight Binding

1 Fold and press the binding as shown and, with right sides together, place it against the raw edge of the main fabric. Machine-stitch the binding along the fold line nearer the edge.

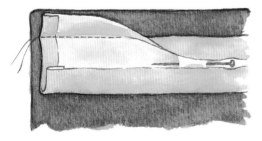

2 Fold the binding over the raw edge to the wrong side of the main fabric and slipstitch in place. Slipstitch the binding neatly at each end.

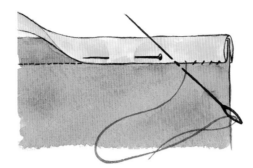

Bias Binding

1 Fold the piece of fabric so that the selvage is parallel to the weft, or cross grain. Press the fold and cut along it. Draw a series of lines parallel to the diagonal cut line, spacing them ½ inch (1 cm) wider than the finished binding. Cut along the lines.

2 Place two strips at right angles and stitch together ¼ inch (5 mm) from the edge.

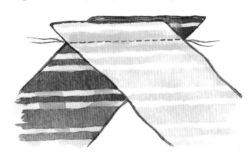

3 Press the seam open and trim away the points of fabric. Apply to the fabric as for straight binding.

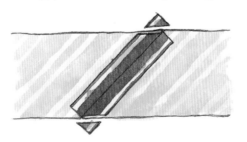

Mitering Binding

1 Mitering binding enables you to apply it around a corner. Place binding against the edge of the fabric with right sides facing. Machine-stitch along one edge to the corner point of the seamline. At the corner, fold the binding back over the stitched length so that the fold is in line with the stitching. Stitch the binding along the second edge.

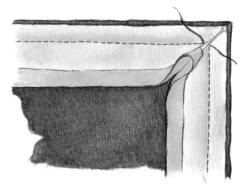

2 Continue to fold back the binding like this at each corner. Turn the binding over the raw edge of the fabric and hand-stitch the other side of the binding to the fabric. Press the corners into miters on both sides by tucking under the fabric.

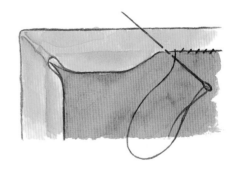

PIPING

Piping is made by inserting cord into binding strips. The width of the binding should equal the circumference of the cord plus 1¼ inches (3 cm) of seam allowance. Wrap the binding around the cord and pin it in place. Sew the fabric together close to the cord, using the zipper foot. Place the piping against the raw edge of the main fabric and stitch.

Glossary

Appliqué Applying a second layer of fabric onto a base cloth, usually with decorative stitching.

Architrave The molding around a window or doorway.

Backstitch A firm hand stitch that resembles machine stitching on the right side of the fabric and overlaps on the wrong side.

Balloon shade A shade consisting of vertical rows of horizontally gathered fabric that may be drawn up to form a series of ruches.

Basting Large straight stitches for temporarily fastening layers of fabric. The thread is usually made of cotton and worked in a loose stitch.

Bay window A window projecting from the wall to form an alcove.

Bias binding A strip of fabric cut obliquely from selvage to selvage for additional strength. Used to bind fabric edges and to enclose piping.

Bow window A bay window in the shape of a curve.

Bracket A decorative support, often made from metal or wood, that holds a curtain or drapery in place.

Braid A woven ribbon for trimming or edging draperies or accessories.

Brocade A woven fabric using silk, wool, cotton, or mixed fibers. Often washable.

Café curtain An informal curtain with a scalloped heading. Often hung halfway down the window.

Cascade The piece of fabric that falls from the end of a swag.

Catchstitch A hemming stitch that is used over any raw edge which is then covered by another fabric.

Chintz Glazed cotton in plain colors or prints. Ideal for curtains, draperies, valances, shades, and bed furnishings. Dry-clean only or the glaze will eventually wash out.

Cornice A horizontal molding at the top of a wall or a decorative board, often molded or painted, that is fixed to the top of the window.

Corona drape A drapery that hangs from a pole or a semicircular bracket (often known as a coronet) at the top of the bed.

Cotton A natural fiber made from the boll of the cotton plant to produce a strong durable yarn. There are a variety of cotton fabrics available, including Madras cotton, a fine striped Indian cotton, usually in bright colors, and cretonne, a heavy cotton cloth. Organdie is also made with cotton yarns.

Crewel Plain or woven cotton or linen with cream or multicolored embroidery that is usually in wool. Crewel is ideal for heavy curtains or draperies or for soft shades. It is often washable but you should check for color fastness first, particularly if the crewel-work is in wool.

Curtain An informal window covering, usually made with a casing, which slips over a rod. Curtains may also be hung from rings.

Damask A reversible figured woven fabric usually made from silk, satin, or linen. Dry-clean only.

Drapery Window covering with (usually) pleated headings which may be lined or unlined. They are usually hung from a traverse rod so that they can be drawn.

Facing A strip of fabric used to hide the raw edge of main fabric, especially on unlined curtains or draperies.

Figured material A fabric with a pattern formed by the structure of the weave.

Finial A decorative fixture attached to the end of a curtain or drapery rod or pole. Available in a range of styles.

Flat seam A simple seam for sewing two pieces of fabric together.

French seam A self-neatening seam to enclose raw edges. Use lightweight fabrics or if a seam will be visible.

Fringe A decorative edging with hanging threads or tassels.

Gathers Folds or puckers created by drawing on loosely stitched thread; hence, running stitch, which is used for gathering fabric or for basting.

Gimp A twist of fabric, sometimes stiffened with cord or wire.

Gingham A plain weave cotton cloth usually woven in stripes or checks. It is suitable for informal curtains.

Grain The pattern of lines on a fabric depending on the weave.

Heading The finish at the top of a curtain or drapery, ranging from simple gathers to pleats and swags. Although many heading styles can be achieved using pleater tapes, hand-sewn headings are more professional.

Hem The border or cut edge of cloth, usually turned under and sewn in place.

Holland linen A hard-wearing, fade-resistant fabric stiffened with oil or shellac. It is particularly useful for valances and shades. Holland can also be made from cotton.

Interfacing Special material for lining and stiffening. It is either sewn or ironed in place.

Interlining A soft but thick fabric in white or off-white that adds bulk to and improves the hang of draperies, valances, swags and cascades. Also acts as an extra layer of insulation. Often known as bump or domette. Dry-clean only.

Lambrequin An ornamental hanging that covers the upper part of a window or door.

Lapped seam A useful seam for matching the pattern on the right sides of two pieces of fabric.

Lawn A fine fabric made from linen or cotton.

Linen Fibers spun from flax to produce a strong but flexible fabric.

Lining Plain cotton with a slight satin weave originally only in white or off-white but now available in a range of colors. Clean as for main fabric but wash the lining with the fabric before making the curtains or draperies to prevent uneven shrinkage.

Lit à la polonaise Drapes that fall from a central point above a bed.

Lock stitch A loose stitch that allows for a degree of movement. Ideal for holding together fabrics, linings, and interlinings.

Miter The diagonal join of two pieces of fabric formed at a corner; hence mitered corners.

Muslin A sheer, strong but delicately woven fabric in white or off-white that can be dyed with pastel colors. Ideal for undercurtains and sheers. Most muslin can withstand a gentle wash but will sometimes shrink and need ironing in order to regain its shape.

Notch A small V-shaped cut in the edge of a fabric.

Passementerie A term to describe a range of decorative trimmings such as gimp, cord, beads, and braid.

Pleat A double fold or crease, pressed or stitched in place.

Pleat tape A tape that is purpose-made to create a particular heading styles.

Portière A curtain or drapery hung in a doorway.

Raw edge The cut edge of fabric, without selvage or hem.

Recess The area of wall around a window when it is set in from the main wall.

Rod casing A type of curtain heading in which a pocket of material is left open at both ends to receive a curtain rod or pole.

Roman shade A shade operated by vertical cords at the back. The fabric draws up into neat folds.

Ruffle A gathered strip of cloth used as a decorative trimming.

Satin A silk, cotton, or synthetic fabric with a smooth, glossy surface and a dull back. Suitable for curtains, valances, shades, and draperies. Wash or dry-clean.

Seam allowance The narrow strip of raw-edged fabric left when making a seam to allow for fraying.

Seamline The line formed when fabric pieces are stitched together.

Selvage The defined warp edge of the fabric, specially woven to prevent unraveling.

Silk A luxuriously strong fabric that is produced by silkworms. There are a variety of silks to choose from, including silk noil, a light- to medium-weight silk, which is ideal for interlining heavy draperies and for making lightweight curtains or draperies. Silk shantung, which has a rather dull appearance, is another light- to medium-weight silk suitable for curtains or draperies. Silks will also provide a further layer of insulation. Dry clean only.

Slipstitch Often used to stitch the folded edge of a lining to the main fabric. Use a color thread to match the main fabric.

Swag Fabric that hangs from two fixed points at the top of the window, and sweeps down in the center to create an elegant curve.

Taffeta A mixed-weave fabric, including silk and acetate, with a reflective sheen. Ideal for extravagant draperies. Dry-clean only.

Template A shape made of card-board or paper and used to mark the specific outlines on a piece of fabric.

Tester A canopy over a four-poster bed; hence, a half-tester.

Tieback A band of fabric used to tie curtains or draperies to one side. Tiebacks may be as simple as a piece of ribbon or brocade or shaped in some way.

Toile A plain cloth or, when described as *toile de Jouy*, one that is embellished with pictorial scenes printed on cotton. Dry-clean only.

Traverse rod A rod with a cord at the side for drawing the curtain or drapery.

Undercurtain The curtain closest to the window in a treatment that includes at least two layers.

Valance A strip of fabric in a variety of styles. Run across the top of a window or along a bed, it is ideal for hiding any structural imperfections.

Velvet A rich fabric with a thick pile, usually made of cotton, silk, or nylon.

Voile A light, plain weave cotton or polyester fabric in a variety of single colors. Suitable for sheer curtains, valances, and bed drapes. Silk and wool voiles are ideal for fine draperies. Washable.

Weave The interlacing action that forms a piece of fabric.

Width The distance from selvage to selvage on any fabric.

Resources

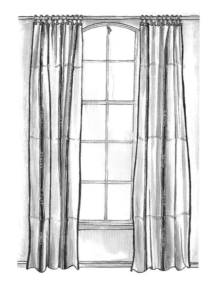

FABRICS

ABC Carpet & Home
881–888 Broadway
New York, NY 10002
212-473-3000
www.abccarpet.com

B & J Fabric
263 West 40th Street
New York, NY 10018
212-354-8150

Brunschwig & Fils
979 Third Avenue
New York, NY 10022
212-838-7878
www.brunschwig.com

Calico Corners
203 Gale Lane
Kennett Square, PA 19348
800-213-6366
www.calicocorners.com

Carlton V Fabrics
979 Third Avenue
New York, NY 10022
212-355-4525

Cath Kidston
201 Mulberry Street
New York, NY 10012
212-343-0223
www.cathkidston.com

Clarence House Fabrics
979 Third Avenue
New York, NY 10022
800-803-2850
www.clarencehouse.com

Colefax & Fowler at
Cowtan & Tout
979 Third Avenue
New York, NY 10022
212-647-6900

Designers Guild at
Osborne & Little
979 Third Avenue
New York, NY 10022
212-751-3333
www.designersguild.com

The Fabric Center
485 Electric Avenue
Fitchburg, MA 01420
508-343-4402

Henry Calvin Fabrics
2046 Lars Way
Medford, Oregon 97501
888-732-1996
www.henrycalvin.com

Hinson & Co. Fabrics
979 Third Avenue
New York, NY 10022
212-688-5538
www.hinsonandcompany.com

J. Robert Scott
979 Third Avenue
New York, NY 10022
212-755-4910
www.jrobertscott.com

Jane Churchill at
Cowtan & Tout
979 Third Avenue
New York, NY 10022
212-647-6900

KA´International
1119–1125 Third Avenue
New York, NY 10021
646-497-1670
www.ka-international.com

Keepsake Quilting
Route 25B
P.O. Box 1618
Center Harbor, NH 03226-1618
800-865-9458

Laura Ashley at
Kravet Fabrics
979 Third Avenue
New York, NY 10022
212-421-6363
www.kravet.com

Lee Jofa
979 Third Avenue
New York, NY 10022
212-688-0444
www.leejofa.com

Nicole Fabre Textiles
www.nicolefabredesigns.com

Nordic Style
www.nordicstyle.com

Oppenheim's
P.O. Box 29
120 East Main Street
North Manchester
IN 46962-0052
800-461-6728

Osborne & Little
979 Third Avenue
New York, NY 10022
212-751-3333
www.osborneandlittle.com

Pierre Deux
570 Madison Avenue
New York, NY 10021
212-570-9343

Ralph Lauren Home
867 Madison Avenue
New York, NY 10021
888-475-7674
www.rlhome.polo.com

Sanderson
979 Third Avenue
New York, NY 10022
212-319-7220
www.sanderson-online.co.uk

Scalamandre Fabrics
222 East 59th Street
New York, NY 10022
212-980-3888
www.scalamandre.com

Schumacher & Co.
979 Third Avenue
New York, NY 10022
800-332-3384
www.fschumacher.com

Smith & Noble
P.O. Box 1387
Corona, CA 91718
800-248-8888

Thai Silks!
252 State Street
Los Altos, CA 94022
800-722-7455

Travers Fabrics
979 Third Avenue
New York, NY 10022
212- 888-7900
www.traversinc.com

V.V. Rouleaux
www.vvrouleaux.com

Waverly Fabrics
www.waverly.com

Westgate Fabrics
905 Avenue T, Suite 905
Grand Prairie, TX 75053
800-527-2517
www.westgatefabrics.com

Zoffany
979 Third Avenue
New York, NY 10022
212-593-9787
www.zoffany.uk.com

NOTIONS AND TRIMS

C. M. Offray & Sons, Inc.
Route 24
P.O. Box 601
Chester, NJ 07930
908-879-4700

Clothilde, Inc.
2 Sew Smart Way
Stevens Point
WI 54481-8031
800-772-2891

Conso Products
P.O. Box 326
Union, SC 29379
800-845-2431

Hollywood Trims
Prym-Dritz Corporation
P.O. Box 5028
Spartanburg, SC 29304
800-845-4948

Nancy's Notions
P.O. Box 683
Beaver Dam, WI 53916
800-833-0690

Tinsel Trading Co.
47 West 38th Street
New York, NY 10018
212-730-1030

CURTAIN HARDWARE

Country Curtains
The Red Lion Inn
Stockbridge, MA 01262
800-244-6020

Gige Interiors Ltd.
170 South Main Street
Yardley, PA 19067
215-493-8052

General Clutch Corp.
200 Harvard Avenue
Stamford, CT 06902
800-552-5100

Kirsch
P.O. Box 0370
Sturgis, MI 49091
800-528-1407

Rue de France
78 Thomas Street
Newport, RI 02840
800-777-0998

Springs Window Fashions
7549 Graber Road
Middleton, WI 53562
800-521-8071

The Warm Company
954 East Union
Seattle, WA 98122
800-234-9276

WINDOW HARDWARE

Blaine Window Hardware, Inc.
17319 Blaine Drive
Hagerstown, MD 21740
301-797-6500

Home Depot
www.homedepot.com
*Check local telephone directory
or visit website to find a store
near you.*

Materials Unlimited
2 West Michigan Avenue
Ypsilanti, MI 48197
800-299-9462

Renovator's Supply
P.O. Box 2515
Conway, NH 03818
800-659-0203

READY-MADE AND CUSTOM-
MADE CURTAIN SUPPLIERS

Bed, Bath, & Beyond
620 Avenue of the Americas
New York, NY 10011
212-255-3550
www.bedbathandbeyond.com

Castle Draperies
23287 Ventura Boulevard
Woodland Hills, CA 91364
818-883-7273
www.castledraperies.com

Country Curtains
800-456-0321
www.countrycurtains.com

Gracious Home
1220 Third Avenue
New York, NY 10021
212-517-6300
www.gracioushome.com

Jo-Ann
13323 Riverside Drive
Sherman Oaks, CA 91423-2508
818-789-3167
1-800-525-4951 for enquiries
www.joann.com

Lowe's
5200 Franklin Street
Michigan City, IN 46360
219-872-2900
www.lowes.com

Pier One Imports
71 Fifth Avenue
New York, NY 10003
212-206-1911
www.pier1.com

Pottery Barn
600 Broadway
New York, NY 10012
800-922-5507
www.potterybarn.com

Sunshine Drapery Company
11660 Page Service Drive
St. Louis, MO 63146
314-569-2980
www.sunshinedrapery.com

Architects and Designers

key: **a** = above, **b** = below,
c = center, **l** = left, **r** = right.

23 Architecture
S. I. Robertson
318 Kensal Road
London W10 5BZ, UK
+ 44-(0)20-8962-8666
www.23arc.com
Page 9.

Alexander Fairweather
*vintage costume
textiles & accessories*
+ 44-(0)7929-359425
Page 92l.

**Andrew Arnott and
Karin Shack**
art & design
517 High Street, Prahran
Victoria 3181
Australia
Pages 48br, 49s.

Andrew Parr
SJB Interior Design Pty Ltd
25 Coventry Street
South Melbourne
Australia
+ 61-03-9686-2122
Pages 86, 114.

Angela A'Court
artist
orangedawe@hotmail.com
Page 9.

Arne Tengblad
artist
+ 33-4-90-72-38-44
arteng@wanadoo.fr
Pages 101bl, 102br.

Ash Sakula Architects
24 Rosebery Avenue
London EC1R 4SX, UK
+ 44-(0)20-7837-9735
www.ashsak.com
Pages 130l 130br.

Azman Associates
*(formerly Azman Owens
Architects)*
18 Charlotte Road
London EC2A 3PB, UK
+ 44-(0)20-7739-8191
www.azmanowens.com
Page 116b.

Barbara Davis
interior design & textiles
607-264-3673
Page 102al.

Bennison
16 Holbein Place
London SW1W 8NL, UK
+ 44-(0)20-7730-8076
bennisonfabrics@
btinternet.com
www.bennisonfabrics.com
Page 95.

Campion A. Platt
152 Madison Avenue
Suite 900
New York, NY 10016–5424
212-779-3835
www.campionplatt.com
**Pages 20a, 73r, 74–5, 88a,
160br.**

Carden Cunietti
83 Westbourne Park Road
London W2 5QH, UK
office: + 44-(0)20-7229-8559
store: + 44-(0)20-7229-8630
www.carden-cunietti.com
**Pages 88–89a, 89a, 129l,
142al, 154l.**

Carnachan Architects Ltd
33 Bath Street
PO Box 37–717, Parnell
Auckland
New Zealand
+ 64-9-3797-234,
**Pages 113, 123r, 126l, 127al,
127r.**

Charles Rutherfoord
51 The Chase
London SW4 0NP, UK
+ 44-(0)20-7627-0182
**Pages 41ac, 62bl, 68a, 109r,
152br.**

Charlotte Barnes Interiors
26 Stanhope Gardens
London SW7 5QX, UK
+ 44-(0)20-7244-9610
**Pages 29b 36, 100, 152ar,
158ac.**

Charlotte Crosland Interiors
62 St Mark's Road
London W10 6NN, UK
+ 44-(0)20-8960-9442
www.charlottecrosland.com
Pages 70–71, 103ar.

**Christian de Falbe Interior
Design**
The Glasshouse
49a Goldhawk Road
London W12 8QP, UK
+ 44-(0)20-8743-3210
studio@cdef.co.uk
www.cdef.co.uk
Page 156cr.

Christophe Gollut
Alistair Colvin Ltd
116 Fulham Road
London SW3 6HU, UK
+ 44-(0)20-7370-325
www.christophegollut.com
**Pages 44–45, 98ar, 99 158ar,
158cr, 159cr.**

Clare Mosley
*gilding, eglomisé panels &
mirrors, lampbases, finials, &
curtain accessories*
+ 44-(0)20-7708-3123
Pages 2, 14–15.

Constanze von Unruh
Constanze Interior Projects
interior design company
Richmond
Surrey TW10 8PL, UK
+ 44-(0)20-8948-5533
constanze@
constanzeinteriorprojects.com
Page 50–51b.

CR Studio Architects, PC
6 West 18th Street
9th floor
New York, NY 10011
212-989-8187
www.crstudio.com
Page 133r.

Daisy Simon Interiors
*architecte d'interieur
décoration*
55 Cours Mirabeau
Passage Agard
13100 Aix-en-Provence
France
daisy.simonaix@wanadoo.fr
Page 102–103a.

Enrica Stabile
*antiques dealer, interior
decorator, and photographic
stylist*
www.enricastabile.com
shop: L'Utile e il Dilettevole
Via Carlo Maria Maggi 6
20154 Milan
Italy
+ 39-0234-53-60-86
Pages 59ar, 84l, 85, 103b.

Eva Johnson
*interior designer and
distributor of TRIP TRAP
wood floor treatment products*
+ 44-(0)1638-731-362
www.evajohnson.com
Page 84r.

Françoise Dorget
Caravane, 6 Rue Pavée
75004 Paris
France
+ 33-1-44-61-04-20
www.caravane.fr
**Pages 1, 7a, 30–31, 34b, 76b,
77, 129r, 137, 161br.**

Frédéric Méchiche
4 rue de Thorigny
75003 Paris
France
+ 33-1-42-78-78-28
Pages 16, 38–39, 144

French Country Living
antiques & decoration
21 Rue de l'Eglise
06250 Mougins
France
+ 33-4-93-75-53-03
f.c.l.com@wanadoo.fr
Page 82ar.

Gloss Ltd
designers of home accessories
274 Portobello Road
London W10 5TE, UK
+ 44-(0)20-8960-4146
pascale@glossltd.u-net.com
Page 153.

Grethe Meyer
designer and architect MAA
Royal Scandinavia A/S
Smallegade 45
2000 Frederiksberg
Denmark
+ 45-38144848
Page-87br.

Helen Ellery
interior design
The Plot London
77 Compton Street
London EC1V 0BN, UK
+ 44-(0)20-7251-8116
www.theplotlondon.com
Pages 108ar, 150–51, 151r.

Helm Architects
2 Montagu Row
London W1U 6DX, UK
+ 44-(0)20-7224-1884
nh@helmarchitects.com
Page 76a.

**Henry Smith-Miller and
Laurie Hawkinson, Architects**
305 Canal Street
New York, NY 10013
212-966-3875
www.smharch.com
Page 32b.

Hilton McConnico
8 rue Antoine Panier
93170 Bagnolet
Paris
France
Pages 25bl, 65a, 141cl,
160bl.

Idarica Gazzoni
Via Santa Marta 11
20123 Milan
Italy
+ 39-02-869-97251
www.idaricagazzoni.com
Page 59al.

Ilaria Miani
shop: Via Monserrato 35
00186 Rome
Italy
+ 39-0668-33160
ilariamiani@tin.it
*Podere Buon Riposo in Val
d'Orcia is available to rent.*
Pages 104al, 104bl.

Interni Pty Ltd
98 Barcom Avenue
Rushcutters Bay 2011
NSW, Sydney
Australia
+ 61-2-9360-5660
Pages 55b, 87bl, 87ar, 89bl,
107bl, 112c, 115l, 125l,
130ar.

IPL Interiors
25 Bullen Street
London SW11 3ER, UK
+ 44-(0)20-7978-4224
Pages 25al, 47a, 47br, 52,
57, 80, 81bl, 90c, 90br, 91,
96–97, 97ar, 106r, 110–11,
116ar, 117, 125r, 126br,
127cl, 127b, 132a, 132–33a,
138–39a, 149l, 149ar, 159ar,
159bl, 159bc.

Jacqueline Coumans
Le Décor Français
1006 Lexington Avenue
New York, NY 10021
212-734-0032
www.ledecorfrancais.com
info@ledecorfrancais.com
Pages 24bc, 24r, 124, 143br,
157l.

James Biber, AIA
Pentagram Architecture
204 Fifth Avenue
New York, NY 10010
www.pentagram.com
212-683-7000
Page 33.

John F. Saladino
Saladino Group Inc.
200 Lexington Avenue
Suite 1600
New York, NY 10016
www.saladinofurniture.com
212-684-6805
Pages 64, 120, 121al, 139bl,
160ar.

Josephine Macrander
interior designer
+ 31 299 402804
Page 142bl.

Kelly Hoppen Interiors
2 Munden Street
London W14 ORH, UK
+ 44-(0)20-7471-3350
www.kellyhoppen.com
Pages 27, 37, 41l, 43, 53, 54l,
69, 108c, 108br, 134b, 136a,
136b, 147, 155a, 155b.

Ken Foreman
architect
105 Duane Street
New York, NY 10007
212-924-4503
Page 133bl.

Khai Liew Design
166 Magill Road
Norwood
South Australia 5067
Australia
+ 61-618-8362-1076
Pages 46r, 118–19.

**Larcombe & Solomon
Architects**
Level 6, 2 Foveaux Street
Surry Hills 2010
NSW
Australia
+ 61-2-9212-6935
Pages 90l, 90ar.

**Laura Bohn Design
Associates, Inc.**
30 West 26th Street
New York, NY 10010
212-645-3636
Page 107r.

Linum
+ 33-4-90-38-37-38
linum@dial.oleane.com
www.linum-france.com
Pages 101bl, 102br.

Marisa Tadiotto Cavalli
Via Solferino 11
20121 Milan
Italy
+ 39-02-36-51-14-49
marisacavalli@hotmail.com
Page 46l.

Mark Smith
Smithcreative
15 St George's Road
London W4 1AU, UK
+ 44-(0)20-8747-3909
info@smithcreative.net
Pages 42a, 42–43.

Mary Bright, Inc.
636 Broadway
Room 620
New York, NY 10012
212-677-1970
www.marybright.com
Pages 6a, 7a, 32, 33, 34a, 35,
138al, 138br.

Mary Drysdale
Drysdale, Inc.
78 Kalorama Cir NW
Washington DC 20008
202-588-0700
Pages 83, 134–35.

McLean Quinlan Architects
2a Bellevue Parade
London SW17 7EQ, UK
+ 44-(0)20-8767-1633
www.mcleanquinlan.com
Page 123bl.

Milly de Cabrol, Ltd
150 East 72nd Street, Suite 2C
New York, NY 10021
212-717-9317
Pages 22a, 29a, 94bl, 156br,
160al, 162.

**Mireille and Jean Claude
Lothon**
La Cour Beaudeval Antiquities
4 rue des Fontaines
28210 Faverolles
France
+ 33-2-37-51-47-67
Page 152al.

Nordic Style
classic Swedish interiors
109 Lots Road
London SW10 0RN, UK
+ 44-(0)20-7351-1755
www.nordicstyle.com
Pages 92r, 101a, 101br, 116l.

Ogawa/Depardon Architects
137 Varick Street, Suite 404
New York, NY 10013
212-627-7390
www.oda-ny.com
Page 35.

Paul Collier, Architect
209 Rue St Maur
75010 Paris
France
+ 33-1-53-72-49-32
paul.collier@architecte.net
Pages 82al, 132bl, 154–55.

Paul Simmons
bespoke, hand-printed textiles
Timorous Beasties
7 Craigend Place
Anniesland
Glasgow G13 2UN, UK
+ 44-(0)141-959-3331
Page 76a.

Piero Castellini Baldissera
architect
Via della Rocca 5
Milan
Italy
+ 39-02-48005384
studiocastellini@libero.it
Page 104r.

Pierre Frey (UK) Ltd
251–53 Fulham Road
London SW3 6HY, UK
+ 44-(0)20-7376-5599
www.pierrefrey.com
Pages 22b, 23, 25r, 47bl,
66–67, 68bl, 97al, 139cl, 139r.

**Retrouvius Reclamation &
Design**
2A Ravensworth Road
London NW10 5NR, UK
+ 44-(0)20-8960-6060
www.retrouvius.com
Page 76a.

Sabina Fay Braxton
Cloth of Gold
Grennan Watermill
Thomastown
Co Kilkenny, Ireland
+ 353-565-4383
by appointment in New York:
212-535-2587
cofgold@indigo.ie
Pages 60ar, 143l.

Sally Storey
John Cullen Lighting
585 King's Road
London SW6 2EH, UK
+ 44-(0)20-7371-5400
Page 56b.

Sasha Waddell
269 Wandsworth Bridge Road
London SW6 2TX, UK
+ 44-(0)20-7736-0766
Pages 112b, 138acl.

Sequana
64 Avenue de la Motte Picquet
75015 Paris
France
+ 33-1-45-66-58-40
sequana@wanadoo.fr
Page 81r.

Sheila Scholes
designer
+ 44-(0)1480-498-241
Pages 65b, 67, 141ar.

Sian Colley Soft Furnishings
Block E 2B Upper Ringway
Bounds Green
London N11 2UD, UK
+ 44-(0)20-8368-4092
colleysian@hotmail.com
Pages 82b, 145bl, 145r.

Stephanie Hoppen
17 Walton Street
London SW3 2HZ, UK
+ 44-(0)20-7589-3678
www.stephaniehoppen.com
Pages 10–13, 41l, 93ar, 93b,
94al, 94r, 136b, 138cr,
142br, 159br, 161bl.

Stephen Varady Architecture
PO Box 105
St Peters
NSW 2044
Sydney
Australia
+ 61-2-9516-4044
Page 107al.

Studio Aandacht
*art direction & interior produc-
tion*
ben.lambers@studioaandacht.nl
www.studioaandacht.nl
Pages 136c, 141br.

Timney Fowler Design Studio
355 King Street
London W6 9NH, UK
+ 44-(0)20-8748-3010
www.timneyfowler.com
Pages 50al, 50ar, 62ar, 96,
128ar, 128b, 149br, 159al.

Todd Klein, Inc.
27 West 24th Street, Suite 802
New York, NY 10010
212-414-0001
todd@toddklein.com
Pages 58l, 59bl, 62al, 62br.

Todhunter Earle Interiors
interior design company
Chelsea Reach, 1st Floor
79–89 Lots Road
London SW10 0RN
+ 44-(0)20-7349-9999
interiors@todhunterearle.com
www.todhunterearle.com
Pages 20b, 148br, 150ac,
155c, 157r.

Tony Suttle
Woods Baget Pty Ltd
64 Marine Parade, Southport
Queensland 4000
Australia
Page 48l, 48ar.

Vicente Wolf Associates, Inc.
333 West 39th Street
Suite 1001
New York, NY 10018
212-465-0590
Pages 4–5, 20–21, 63, 72,
73l, 81a, 81cl, 89br, 106l,
110b, 121b, 122, 123al, 131,
138bcl, 161ar.

Vincent Dané
interior design antiques
50 Cranby Gardens
London SW7 3DE, UK
Pages 6b, 24l, 24ac, 58r, 93al,
140r, 141al.

**Vivien Lawrence Interior
Design**
interior designer of private homes
+ 44-(0)20-8209-0058
+ 44-(0)020-8209-0562
vl-interiordesign@cwcom.net
Pages 54ar, 152bl.

Voon Wong & Benson Saw
Unit 27
1 Stannary Street, UK
London SE11 4AD
+ 44-(0)020-7587-0116
www.voon-benson.co.uk
Page 55a.

Yves Halard
interior decoration
252 bis Boulevard St Germain
75007 Paris
France
+ 33-01-42-22-60-50
Page 61.

Picture Credits

All photographs by James Merrell unless otherwise stated.

key: **ph** = photographer, **a** = above, **b** = below, **l** = left, **r** = right, **c** = center.

1 Charles Chauliaguet and Françoise Dorget's apartment in Paris by Caravane; **2 ph** Christopher Drake/Clare Mosley's house in London; **3** Sue and Andy A'Court's apartment in Blackheath, London; **4–5** Shelly Washington's apartment designed by Vicente Wolf; **6a** curtain designed by Mary Bright; **6b** designed by Vincent Dané; **7a** designed by Françoise Dorget, Caravane; **7a** curtain designed by Mary Bright; **9** Christopher Drake/a house designed by artist Angela A'Court, extension and alteration to rear of property by S. I. Robertson at 23 Architecture; **10–13** an apartment in London designed by Stephanie Hoppen and executed by Doreen Scott; **14–15 ph** Christopher Drake/Clare Mosley's house in London; **16** Frédéric Méchiche's house near Toulon; **17 ph** Fritz von der Schulenburg/ Jason McCoy's apartment in New York; **18–19** Sue and Andy A'Court's apartment in Blackheath, London; **20a** architect Campion A. Platt; **20b** an apartment in London designed by Emily Todhunter; **20–21** Amy & Richard Sachs' apartment in New York designed by Vicente Wolf; **22a** Milly de Cabrol's apartment in New York; **22b & 23** Mr. & Mrs. Patrick Frey's house in Paris; **24l&ac** Vincent Dané's house near Biarritz; **24bc&r** an apartment in New York designed by Jacqueline Coumans, Le Décor Français with the help of Olivier Gelbsmann; **25al** François Gilles & Dominique Lubar, IPL Interiors; **25bl** Hilton McConnico's house near Paris; **25r** Mr & Mrs Patrick Frey's house in Paris; **27** Kelly Hoppen's apartment in London; **28 ph** Alan Williams/Lisa Fine's apartment in Paris; **29a** Milly Cabrol's apartment in New York; **29b** designed by Charlotte Barnes; **30–31** Charles Chauliaguet and Françoise Dorget's apartment in Paris by Caravane; **32** curtains designed by Mary Bright; **32b** architect Henry Smith–Miller & Laurie Hawkinson, curtain designed by

Mary Bright; **33** an apartment in New York designed by James Biber of Pentagram with curtain design by Mary Bright; **34a** curtain designed by Mary Bright; **34b** Charles Chauliaguet and Françoise Dorget's apartment in Paris by Caravane; **35** architects Ogawa Depardon, curtain designed by Mary Bright; **36** designed by Charlotte Barnes; **37** Kelly Hoppen's apartment in London; **38–39** Frédéric Méchiche's house near Toulon; **40 ph** Simon Upton **41l** a room in Stephanie Hoppen's London apartment designed by Kelly Hoppen and Doreen Scott; **41ac** a house in London designed by Charles Rutherfoord; **41bc&r** Sue and Andy A'Court's apartment in Blackheath, London; **42a & 42–43 ph** Jan Baldwin/Mark Smith's home in the Cotswolds; **42b** designed by Roger Banks-Pye; **43** Kelly Hoppen's apartment in London; **44–45** Christophe Gollut's apartment in London; **46l ph** Christopher Drake/ Marisa Cavalli's home in Milan; **46r** Khai & Sue Kellet; **47a&br** François Gilles & Dominique Lubar, IPL Interiors; **47bl** Mr & Mrs Patrick Frey's house in Paris; **48l&ar** Tony Suttle's house in Brisbane; **48br & 49** Andrew Arnott and Karin Schack's house in Melbourne; **50al&ar** Sue Timney's house in London designed by Timney–Fowler Ltd.; **50–51b ph** Jan Baldwin/ Constanze von Unruh's house in London; **51** an apartment in London designed by Nigel Greenwood; **52** an apartment in London designed by François Gilles & Dominique Lubar, IPL Interiors; **53** Kelly Hoppen's apartment in London; **54l** Kelly Hoppen's apartment in London; **54ar ph** Christopher Drake/Vivien Lawrence an interior designer in London(020 8209 0562); **55a ph** Jan Baldwin/the Campbell family's apartment in London, architecture by Voon Wong Architects; **55b** Interni interior design consultancy; **56b ph** Ray Main/ Alex and Charlie Manners' house in London, lighting designed by Sally Storey, Design Director of John Cullen Lighting; **57** a house in London designed by François Gilles & Dominique Lubar, IPL Interiors; **58l ph** Chris Everard/Todd Klein's New York apartment designed by Todd Klein, Inc.; **58r** Vincent Dané's house near Biarritz; **59al ph** Chris Tubbs/Idarica & Piero Prinetti-

Castelletti's 'Allevamento del Fezzo' in Ottiglio, Alessandria; **59ar ph** Christopher Drake/Enrica Stabile's house in Le Thor, Provence; **59bl ph** Chris Everard/ Todd Klein's New York apartment designed by Todd Klein, Inc.; **60l ph** Ray Main; **60ar ph** David Montgomery/Sabina Fay Braxton's apartment in Paris; **60br ph** Alan Williams/Lisa Fine's apartment in Paris; **61 ph** Alan Williams/interior designer and managing director of the Société Yves Halard, Michelle Halard's own apartment in Paris; **62ar** Sue Timney's house in London designed by Timney–Fowler Ltd.; **62al&br ph** Chris Everard/Todd Klein's New York apartment designed by Todd Klein, Inc.; **62bl** an apartment in London designed by Charles Rutherfoord; **63** Shelly Washington's apartment in New York designed by Vicente Wolf; **64** John F. Saladino's apartment in New York; **65a** Hilton McConnico's house near Paris; **65b ph** David Montgomery/Sheila Scholes' house near Cambridge; **66–67** Mr & Mrs Patrick Frey's house in Paris; **67 ph** Polly Eltes/Sheila Scholes' house near Cambridge; **68a** Charles Rutherfoord's house in London; **68bl** Mr & Mrs Patrick Frey's house in Paris; **68br** Linda Trahair's house in Bath; **69** Kelly Hoppen's apartment in London; **70–71 ph** Polly Eltes/a house in London designed by Charlotte Crosland Interiors; **72** Shelly Washington's apartment in New York designed by Vicente Wolf; **73l** Amy and Richard Sachs' apartment in New York designed by Vicente Wolf; Hotel Villa Gallici, Aix-en-Provence; **73r** architect Campion A. Platt; **74–75** an apartment in New York architect Campion A. Platt; **76a ph** Jan Baldwin/a family home in Parsons Green, London, architecture by Nicholas Helm and Yasuyuki Fukuda (architectural assistant) of Helm Architects, interior design and all material finishes supplied by Maria Speake of Retrouvius Reclamation & Design; **76b & 77** Charles Chauliaguet and Françoise Dorget's apartment in Paris by Caravane; **78l&br** Nigel Greenwood's apartment in London; **78ar ph** Alan Williams/Lisa Fine's apartment in Paris; **79** Nigel Greenwood's apartment in London; **80** a house in London designed by François Gilles & Dominique

Lubar, IPL Interiors; **81a&cl** Amy & Richard Sachs' apartment in New York designed by Vicente Wolf; **81bl** designed by François Gilles & Dominique Lubar, IPL Interiors; **81r ph** Andrew Wood/Mary Shaw's Sequana apartment in Paris; **82al ph** Chris Everard/an apartment in Paris, designed by architect Paul Collier; **82ar ph** Christopher Drake/owners of French Country Living, the Hill family's home on the Côte d'Azur; **82b ph** Polly Eltes/curtain design by Sian and Annie Colley; **84l ph** Christopher Drake/Enrica Stabile's house in Milan; **84r ph** Christopher Drake/Eva Johnson's house in Suffolk, interiors designed by Eva Johnson; **85 ph** Christopher Drake/Sasha Waddell's house in Le Thor, Provence; **86** Andrew Parr's house in Melbourne; **87al ph** Henry Bourne; **87br ph** Andrew Wood/architect Grethe Meyer's house, Hørsholm, Denmark, built by architects Moldenhawer, Hammer and Frederiksen, 1963; **87bl&ar** Interni interior design consultancy; **88a** an apartment in New York architect Campion A. Platt; **88b** Sarah Elson's house in London; **88–89a & 89a ph** Polly Eltes/Debby & Jeremy Amias' house in London designed by Carden Cunietti; **89bl** Interni interior design consultancy; **89br** Amy & Richard Sachs' apartment in New York designed by Vicente Wolf; **90l&ar** Larcombe and Solomon; **90cr&br & 91** a house in London designed by François Gilles & Dominique Lubar, IPL Interiors; **92l ph** Catherine Gratwicke/Rose Hammick's home in London–1950s curtains from Alexandra Fairweather; **92r ph** Christopher Drake/Nordic Style kitchen; **93al** Vincent Dané's house near Biarritz; **93ar&b** an apartment in London designed by Stephanie Hoppen and executed by Doreen Scott; **94al&r** an apartment in London designed by Stephanie Hoppen and executed by Doreen Scott; **94bl** an apartment in New York designed by Milly de Cabrol; **95 ph** Alan Williams/the Norfolk home of Geoff & Gilly Newberry of Bennison Fabrics, all fabrics by Bennison–on sofa: Trincomalee in pink and green on beige linen; curtains: Tulip Tree in pink and green on beige linen; **96** Sue Timney's house in London designed by Timney–Fowler Ltd; **96–97 & 97ar** an apartment in London designed by François Gilles & Dominique Lubar, IPL Interiors; **97al** Mr. & Mrs. Patrick Frey's house in Paris; **98all except 98ar** Sue & Andy A'Court's apartment in Blackheath, London; **98ar & 99** Christophe Gollut's apartment in London; **100** designed by Charlotte Barnes; **101a&br ph** Christopher Drake/Nordic Style bedroom; **101bl ph** Christopher Drake/Anna Bonde and artist Arne Tengblad's home in the Luberon Valley, Provence; **102al ph** Christopher Drake/designer Barbara Davis' own house in upstate New York; **102br ph** Christopher Drake/Anna Bonde and artist Arne Tengblad's home in the Luberon Valley, Provence; **102–103a ph** Christopher Drake/a family home near Aix-en-Provence with interior design by Daisy Simon; **103ar ph** Polly Eltes/a house in London designed by Charlotte Crosland Interiors; **103b ph** Christopher Drake/Enrica Stabile's house in Brunello; **104al&bl ph** Chris Tubbs/Giorgio & Ilaria Miani's Podere Buon Riposo in Val d'Orcia; **104r ph** Chris Tubbs/a house in Tuscany planned and decorated by architect Piero Castellini; **105 ph** Debi Treloar/Cristine Tholstrup Hermansen and Helge Drenck's house in Copenhagen; **106l** Shelly Washington's apartment in New York designed by Vicente Wolf; **106r** London house designed by François Gilles & Dominique Lubar, IPL Interiors; **107al** Amanda and Andrew Manning's apartment in Sydney designed by Stephen Varady; **107bl** designed by Interni interior design consultancy; **107r ph** David Montgomery/Laura Bohn's apartment

in New York designed by Laura Bohn Design Associates; **108l** designed by Cath Kidston; **108ar ph** Christopher Drake/a house in Salisbury designed by Helen Ellery of The Plot London; **108c&br** Kelly Hoppen's apartment in London; **109l** Sarah Elson's house in London; **109r** an apartment in London designed by Charles Rutherfoord; **110a ph** Debi Treloar; **110b** Amy & Richard Sachs' apartment in New York designed by Vicente Wolf; **110–11** a house in London designed by François Gilles & Dominique Lubar, IPL Interiors; **112c** Interni interior design consultancy; **112b ph** David Montgomery/Sasha Waddell's house in London; **113** Robyn & Simon Carnachan's house in Auckland; **114** Andrew Parr's house in Melbourne; **115l** Interni interior design consultancy; **115r ph** Christopher Drake; **116l ph** Christopher Drake/Nordic Style bedroom **116ar** a house in London designed by François Gilles & Dominique Lubar, IPL Interiors; **116b ph** Andrew Wood/Guido Palau's house in North London, designed by Azman Owens Architects; **117** a house in London designed by François Gilles & Dominique Lubar, IPL Interiors; **118–19** Khai Liew and Sue Kellet's house in Adelaide; **120** John F. Saladino's apartment, New York; **121al** John F. Saladino's apartment, New York; **121b** Amy & Richard Sachs' apartment, New York designed by Vicente Wolf; **122** Vicente Wolf's apartment, New York; **123al** Amy & Richard Sachs' apartment, New York designed by Vicente Wolf; **123bl ph** Christopher Drake/designed by McLean Quinlan Architects; **123r** Robyn & Simon Carnachan's house in Auckland; **124** an apartment in New York designed by Jacqueline Coumans, Le Décor Français with the help of Olivier Gelbsmann; **125l** Interni interior design consultancy; **125r** an apartment in London designed by François Gilles & Dominique Lubar, IPL Interiors; **126l** Robyn & Simon Carnachan's house in Auckland; **126ar** Jolie and Petra Grant's house in Brisbane; **126br ph** Polly Eltes/a house in London designed by François Gilles and Dominique Lubar of IPL Interiors; **127al&r** Robyn & Simon Carnachan's house in Auckland; **127cl&b** an apartment in London designed by François Gilles & Dominique Lubar, IPL Interiors; **128al** John Raab's apartment in London; 128ar&b Sue Timney's house in London designed by Timney–Fowler Ltd.; **129l ph** Polly Eltes/Debby & Jeremy Amias' house in London designed by Carden Cunietti; **129r** Charles Chauliaguet and Françoise Dorget's apartment in Paris by Caravane; **130l&br** an apartment in London designed by Ash Sakula Architects; **130ar** designed by Interni interior design consultancy; **131** Vicente Wolf's apartment in New York; **132a & 132–33a** an apartment in London designed by François Gilles & Dominique Lubar, IPL Interiors; **132bl ph** Chris Everard/an apartment in Paris, designed by architect Paul Collier; **132br** Bellevue Homestead, Coominya, a NT of Queensland Property; **133bl ph** David Montgomery/an apartment in New York designed by Ken Foreman; **133r ph** David Montgomery/the House of Crypton living laboratory apartment showroom in New York City designed by CR Studio Architects, PC; **134a** Sue and Andy A'Court; **134b** designed by Kelly Hoppen; **136a** designed by Kelly Hoppen; **136c ph** Debi Treloar/the home of Studio Aandacht, design by Ben Lambers; **136b** a room in Stephanie Hoppen's London apartment designed by Kelly Hoppen and Doreen Scott; **137** Charles Chauliaguet and Françoise Dorget's apartment in Paris by Caravane; **138al&br** curtain designed by Mary Bright; **138acl ph** David Montgomery/Sasha

Waddell's house in London; **138bcl** designed by Vicente Wolf; **138cr** designed by Stephanie Hoppen and executed by Doreen Scott; **138–39a** designed by François Gilles & Dominique Lubar, IPL Interiors; **139cl&r** Mr & Mrs Patrick Frey's house in Paris; **139bl** designed by John F. Saladino; **140l** Christian Sarramon; **140r & 141al** designed by Vicente Dané; **141ar ph** David Montgomery/Sheila Scholes' house near Cambridge; **141cl** designed by Hilton McConnico; **141br ph** Debi Treloar/the home of Studio Aandacht, design by Ben Lambers; **142al ph** Polly Eltes/Debby & Jeremy Amias' house in London designed by Carden Cunietti; **142ar** designed by Cath Kidston; **142bl ph** Debi Treloar/Wim and Josephine's apartment in Amsterdam; **142br** designed by Stephanie Hoppen and executed by Doreen Scott; **143al** Sarah Elson; **143ar** Sue and Andy A'Court; **143l ph** David Montgomery/Sabina Fay Braxton's apartment in Paris; **143br** designer Jacqueline Coumans, Le Décor Français; **144** a house in Toulon designed by Frédéric Méchiche; **145al&cl** designed by Katrin Cargill; **145bl&r ph** Polly Eltes/curtain design by Sian and Annie Colley; **147** Kelly Hoppen's apartment in London; **148br ph** Polly Eltes/Emily Todhunter's house in London designed by Todhunter Earle Interiors; **149l&ar** a house in London designed by François Gilles & Dominique Lubar, IPL Interiors; **149br** Sue Timney's house, London designed by Timney–Fowler Ltd.; **150ac ph** David Montgomery/a house in South London designed by Todhunter Earle Interiors; **150–51 ph** Chris Everard/a house in London designed by Helen Ellery of The Plot London; **151r ph** Christopher Drake/a house in Salisbury designed by Helen Ellery of The Plot London; **152al ph** Christopher Drake/owners of La Cour Beaudeval Antiquities, Mireille and Jean Claude Lothon's house in Faverolles; **152bl ph** Christopher Drake/Vivien Lawrence an interior designer in London (020 8209 0562); **152ar** designed by Charlotte Barnes; **152br** designed by Charles Rutherfoord; **153 ph** Alan Williams/owner of Gloss, Pascale Bredillet's own apartment in London; **154l ph** Polly Eltes/Debby & Jeremy Amias' house in London designed by Carden Cunietti; **154ac** Sue and Andy A'Court; **154–55 ph** Chris Everard/an apartment in Paris, designed by architect Paul Collier; **155a&b** designed by Kelly Hoppen; **155c ph** David Montgomery/a house in South London designed by Todhunter Earle Interiors; **156l** Sue and Andy A'Court's home in Blackheath, London; **156cr ph** Polly Eltes/Christian de Falbe's London home; **156br** designed by Milly de Cabrol; **157l** designed by Jacqueline Coumans, Le Décor Français; **157r ph** Polly Eltes/Emily Todhunter's house in London designed by Todhunter Earle Interiors; **158ac** designed by Charlotte Barnes; **158cl** designed by Tomasz Starzewski; **158ar&cr** designed by Christophe Gollut; **158b** Bellevue Homestead, Coominya, a NT of Queensland Property; **159al** designed by Timney–Fowler Ltd; **159ar** designed by François Gilles and Dominique Lubar, IPL Interiors; **159c** designed by Katrin Cargill; **159cr** designed by Christophe Gollut; **159bl&bc** designed by François Gilles & Dominique Lubar, IPL Interiors; **159br** designed by Stephanie Hoppen and executed by Doreen Scott; **160al** Milly de Cabrol; **160ar** John F. Saladino; **160bl** Hilton McConnico; **160br** designed by Campion A. Platt; **161al** Sarah Elson; **161ar** designed by Vicente Wolf; **161bl** designed by Stephanie Hoppen and executed by Doreen Scott; **161br** Françoise Dorget's apartment; **162** Milly de Cabrol's apartment in NY.

Index

Author's Acknowledgments

Writing a book on such a vast subject is a daunting task. However, the writing of

Curtains: A Design Source Book was made much easier by all the help that I was given by those who know

much more than I do. I would like to thank, in particular, Corleen Rathbone, who is an exceptional curtain-

maker and was more than generous with her time and knowledge, and everyone at Ryland Peters & Small.